COMPUTER PROGRAMMING
(THEORY AND PRACTICALS)

AUTHOR

Dr. Satyendra Singh Chouhan
Assistant Professor,
Department of Computer Science and Engineering
Malaviya National Institute of Technology
Jaipur-302017, Rajasthan

REVIEWER

Prof (Dr.) Kusum Deep
Professor (HAG)
Department of Mathematics
Indian Institute of Technology
Roorkee-247667, Uttarakhand

KHANNA BOOK PUBLISHING CO. (P) Ltd.
4C/4344, Ansari Road, Darya Ganj,
New Delhi, India

All India Council for Technical Education
Nelson Mandela Marg, Vasant Kunj,
New Delhi, India

Dear Readers,

To prevent the piracy, this book is secured with HIGH SECURITY HOLOGRAM on the front title cover. In case you don't find the hologram on the front cover title, please write us to at contact@khannabooks.com or whatsapp us at +91-99109 09320 and avail special gift voucher for yourself.

Specimen of Hologram on front Cover title:

Moreover, there is a SPECIAL DISCOUNT COUPON for you with EVERY HOLOGRAM.

How to avail this SPECIAL DISCOUNT:

Step 1: Scratch the hologram

Step 2: Under the scratch area, your "coupon code" is available

Step 3: Logon to www.khannabooks.com

Step 4: Use your "coupon code" in the shopping cart and get your copy at a special discount

Step 5: Enjoy your reading!

ISBN: 978-93-5538-267-2
Book Code: DIP442EN

Computer Programming: Theory and Practicals

by Dr. Satyendra Singh Chouhan

First Edition: 2026

Originally Published by:
All India Council for Technical Education, Ministry of Education, GOI

Exclusively Published & Distributed by:
Khanna Book Publishing Co. (P) Ltd.
4C/4344, Ansari Road, Daryaganj,
New Delhi (INDIA)

Visit us at: **www.khannabooks.com**
Write us at: **contact@khannabooks.com**

To view complete list of books, Please scan the QR Code:

KPH

Printed in Bharat.

प्रो. टी. जी. सीताराम
अध्यक्ष
Prof. T. G. Sitharam
Chairman

सत्यमेव जयते

आज़ादी का अमृत महोत्सव

अखिल भारतीय तकनीकी शिक्षा परिषद्
(भारत सरकार का एक सांविधिक निकाय)
(शिक्षा मंत्रालय, भारत सरकार)
नेल्सन मंडेला मार्ग, वसंत कुंज, नई दिल्ली–110070
दूरभाष : 011–26131498
ई–मेल : chairman@aicte-india.org

ALL INDIA COUNCIL FOR TECHNICAL EDUCATION
(A STATUTORY BODY OF THE GOVT. OF INDIA)
(Ministry of Education, Govt. of India)
Nelson Mandela Marg, Vasant Kunj, New Delhi-110070
Phone : 011-26131498
E-mail : chairman@aicte-india.org

FOREWORD

Engineers are the backbone of any modern society. They are the ones responsible for the marvels as well as the improved quality of life across the world. Engineers have driven humanity towards greater heights in a more evolved and unprecedented manner.

The All India Council for Technical Education (AICTE), have spared no efforts towards the strengthening of the technical education in the country. AICTE is always committed towards promoting quality Technical Education to make India a modern developed nation emphasizing on the overall welfare of mankind.

An array of initiatives has been taken by AICTE in last decade which have been accelerated now by the National Education Policy (NEP) 2020. The implementation of NEP under the visionary leadership of Hon'ble Prime Minister of India envisages the provision for education in regional languages to all, thereby ensuring that every graduate becomes competent enough and is in a position to contribute towards the national growth and development through innovation & entrepreneurship.

One of the spheres where AICTE had been relentlessly working since past couple of years is providing high quality original technical contents at Under Graduate & Diploma level prepared and translated by eminent educators in various Indian languages to its aspirants. For students pursuing 2nd year of their Engineering education, AICTE has identified 87 books, which shall be translated into 12 Indian languages - Hindi, Tamil, Gujarati, Odia, Bengali, Kannada, Urdu, Punjabi, Telugu, Marathi, Assamese & Malayalam. In addition to the English medium, books in different Indian Languages are going to support the students to understand the concepts in their respective mother tongue.

On behalf of AICTE, I express sincere gratitude to all distinguished authors, reviewers and translators from the renowned institutions of high repute for their admirable contribution in a record span of time.

AICTE is confident that these outcomes based original contents shall help aspirants to master the subject with comprehension and greater ease.

(Prof. T. G. Sitharam)

ACKNOWLEDGEMENT

The authors are grateful to the authorities of AICTE, particularly Prof. T. G. Sitharam, Chairman; Prof. M. P. Poonia, Vice-Chairman; Prof. Rajive Kumar, Member-Secretary and Dr Amit Kumar Srivastava, Director, Faculty Development Cell for their planning to publish the books on Computer Programming: Theory and Practicals. We sincerely acknowledge the valuable contributions of the reviewer of the book Prof (Dr.) Kusum Deep, Professor (HAG),Department of Mathematics, Indian Institute of Technology Roorkee, for making it students' friendly and giving a better shape in an artistic manner.

I would like to acknowledge and thankmy students at MNIT Jaipur specially, Praveen Singh Thakur, Jitendra Parmar, and Aditi Seetha for their constant support without which book would not have been completed. I would like to express my deepest gratitude to my parents and my family for being supportive. I would also like to express my thanks to my brother Vikram for always being there by my side and keeping faith on me. Finally, this book is dedicated to my wife Sonali and children Prathvi, Samarth & Niyati.

This book is an outcome of various suggestions of AICTE members, experts and authors who shared their opinion and thought to further develop the engineering education in our country. Acknowledgements are due to the contributors and different workers in this field whose published books, review articles, papers, photographs, footnotes, references and other valuable information enriched us at the time of writing the book.

Satyendra Singh Chouhan

PREFACE

The book titled "Computer Programming: Theory and Practicals" is an outcome of the experience of my teaching ofvarious computer programming courses. The initiation of writing this book is to expose fundamentals of computer programming to the engineering students, and usages of C language to solve computation problems. Keeping in mind the purpose of wide coverage as well as to provide essential supplementary information, we have included the topics recommended by AICTE, in a very systematic and orderly manner throughout the book. Efforts have been made to explain the fundamental concepts of the subject in the simplest possible way.

During the process of preparation of the manuscript, we have considered the various standard textbooks and accordingly sections like questions, Notes,problems solved and supplementary problems etc are developed. While preparing the different sections, emphasis has also been laid on motivation behind the topics covered through real world examples and why it is useful in computational problem solving. The book covers all types of medium and advanced level problems and these have been presented in a very logical and systematic manner. The gradations of those problems have been tested over many years of teaching to a wide variety of students.

Apart from illustrations and examples as required, the book is also enriched with numerous programming codes in every unit for proper understanding of the related topics. In this book, various programming tips also given in form of highlighted notes.It included the relevant programming practicals and further links for video lectures that explains the programming examples. A supplementary material, a dedicated video lecture series is also created. The link for the same is provided at the end of the unit. In addition, besides some essential information for the users under the heading "Know More" we have clarified some essential basic information in the appendix and annexure section.

As far as the present book is concerned, "Computer Programming: Theory and Practicals" is meant to provide a thorough grounding in programming fundamentals using C Language. This book will prepare engineering/diploma students to apply the knowledge of computer programming to tackle 21st century and onward computation problem solving. The subject matters are presented in a constructive manner so that an Engineering degree prepares students to work in different sectors or in national laboratories at the very forefront of computer technology.

I sincerely hope that the book will inspire the students to learn and discuss the ideas behind basic principles of Problem Solving using C programming language and will surely contribute to the development of a solid foundation of the subject. We would be thankful to all beneficial comments and suggestions which will contribute to the improvement of the future editions of the book. It gives us immense pleasure to place this book in the hands of the teachers and students. It was indeed a big pleasure to work on different aspects covering in the book.

Satyendra Singh Chouhan

OUTCOME BASED EDUCATION

For the implementation of an outcome based education the first requirement is to develop an outcome based curriculum and incorporate an outcome based assessment in the education system. By going through outcome based assessments, evaluators will be able to evaluate whether the students have achieved the outlined standard, specific and measurable outcomes. With the proper incorporation of outcome based education there will be a definite commitment to achieve a minimum standard for all learners without giving up at any level. At the end of the programme running with the aid of outcome based education, a student will be able to arrive at the following outcomes:

Programme Outcomes (POs) are statements that describe what students are expected to know and be able to do upon graduating from the program. These relate to the skills, knowledge, analytical ability attitude and behaviour that students acquire through the program. The POs essentially indicate what the students can do from subject-wise knowledge acquired by them during the program. As such, POs define the professional profile of an engineering diploma graduate.

National Board of Accreditation (NBA) has defined the following seven POs for an Engineering diploma graduate:

PO1. Basic and Discipline specific knowledge: Apply knowledge of basic mathematics, science and engineering fundamentals and engineering specialization to solve the engineering problems.

PO2. Problem analysis: Identify and analyses well-defined engineering problems using codified standard methods.

PO3. Design/ development of solutions: Design solutions for well-defined technical problems and assist with the design of systems components or processes to meet specified needs.

PO4. Engineering Tools, Experimentation and Testing: Apply modern engineering tools and appropriate technique to conduct standard tests and measurements.

PO5. Engineering practices for society, sustainability and environment: Apply appropriate technology in context of society, sustainability, environment and ethical practices.

PO6. Project Management: Use engineering management principles individually, as a team member or a leader to manage projects and effectively communicate about well-defined engineering activities.

PO7. Life-long learning: Ability to analyse individual needs and engage in updating in the context of technological changes.

COURSE OUTCOMES (CO)

By the end of the course the students are expected to learn:

CO-1: Illustrate and explain the basic computer concepts and programming principles.

CO-2: Learn problem-solving through Computer programming.

CO-3: Formulate a solution for a given problem as a well-defined sequence of actions.

CO-4: Translate the sequence of steps (Algorithms) to C programs.

CO-5: Decompose a problem into functions and synthesize a complete program.

CO-6: Design solutions to engineering problems by applying the basic programming principles of C language.

Mapping of Course Outcomes with Programme Outcomes to be done according to the matrix given below:

Course Outcomes	EXPECTED MAPPING WITH PROGRAMME OUTCOMES (1- Weak Correlation; 2- Medium correlation; 3- Strong Correlation)						
	PO-1	PO-2	PO-3	PO-4	PO-5	PO-6	PO-7
CO-1	3	3	1	2	1	1	3
CO-2	3	2	2	3	1	1	3
CO-3	2	3	3	2	1	1	3
CO-4	2	3	3	3	1	1	3
CO-5	2	3	3	3	1	1	3
CO-6	2	2	3	3	1	2	3

GUIDELINES FOR TEACHERS

To implement Outcome Based Education (OBE) knowledge level and skill set of the students should be enhanced. Teachers should take a major responsibility for the proper implementation of OBE. Some of the responsibilities (not limited to) for the teachers in OBE system may be as follows:

- Within reasonable constraint, they should manoeuvre time to the best advantage of all students.
- They should assess the students only upon certain defined criterion without considering any other potential ineligibility to discriminate them.
- They should try to grow the learning abilities of the students to a certain level before they leave the institute.
- They should try to ensure that all the students are equipped with the quality knowledge as well as competence after they finish their education.
- They should always encourage the students to develop their ultimate performance capabilities.
- They should facilitate and encourage group work and team work to consolidate newer approach.
- They should follow Blooms taxonomy in every part of the assessment.

Bloom's Taxonomy

Level	Teacher should Check	Student should be able to	Possible Mode of Assessment
Creating	Students ability to create	Design or Create	Mini project
Evaluating	Students ability to Justify	Argue or Defend	Assignment
Analysing	Students ability to distinguish	Differentiate or Distinguish	Project/Lab Methodology
Applying	Students ability to use information	Operate or Demonstrate	Technical Presentation/ Demonstration
Understanding	Students ability to explain the ideas	Explain or Classify	Presentation/Seminar
Remembering	Students ability to recall (or remember)	Define or Recall	Quiz

GUIDELINES FOR STUDENTS

Students should take equal responsibility for implementing the OBE. Some of the responsibilities (not limited to) for the students in OBE system are as follows:

- Students should be well aware of each UO before the start of a unit in each and every course.
- Students should be well aware of each CO before the start of the course.
- Students should be well aware of each PO before the start of the programme.
- Students should think critically and reasonably with proper reflection and action.
- Learning of the students should be connected and integrated with practical and real life consequences.
- Students should be well aware of their competency at every level of OBE.

ABBREVIATIONS AND SYMBOLS

List of Abbreviations

General Terms			
Abbreviations	**Full form**	**Abbreviations**	**Full form**
ALU	Arithmetic logic unit	LIFO	Last In First Out
AMD	Advanced Micro Devices	MCQs	Multiple Choice Questions
AOCC	AMD Optimizing C/C++ Compiler	MSVC	Microsoft Visual C++
		PCCM	portable C compiler machine
CPU	Central Processing Unit	QR code	Quick response code
FIFO	First In Fast Out	RAM	Random-access memory
GCD	Greatest Common Divisor	TCC	Tiny C Compiler
IDE	Integrated development environment		

List of Units and Symbols

<table>
<tr><th>Symbols</th><th>Description</th><th>Symbols</th><th>Description</th></tr>
<tr><td>&</td><td>Ampersand</td><td>#</td><td>Hash symbol</td></tr>
<tr><td>`</td><td>Apostrophe</td><td><</td><td>Opening angle bracket</td></tr>
<tr><td>*</td><td>Asterisk</td><td>%</td><td>Percent sign</td></tr>
<tr><td>\</td><td>Backslash</td><td>.</td><td>Period</td></tr>
<tr><td>^</td><td>Caret</td><td>+</td><td>Plus sign</td></tr>
<tr><td>></td><td>Closing angle bracket</td><td>?</td><td>Question mark</td></tr>
<tr><td>:</td><td>Colon</td><td>"</td><td>Quotation mark</td></tr>
<tr><td>,</td><td>Comma</td><td>}</td><td>Right brace</td></tr>
<tr><td>$</td><td>Dollar sign</td><td>]</td><td>Right bracket</td></tr>
<tr><td>=</td><td>Equal to sign</td><td>)</td><td>Right parenthesis</td></tr>
<tr><td>!</td><td>Exclamation mark</td><td>:</td><td>Semicolon</td></tr>
<tr><td>{</td><td>Left brace</td><td>/</td><td>Forward Slash</td></tr>
<tr><td>[</td><td>Left bracket</td><td>~</td><td>Tilde</td></tr>
<tr><td>(</td><td>Lest parenthesis</td><td>_</td><td>Underscore</td></tr>
<tr><td>–</td><td>Minus sign</td><td>|</td><td>Vertical bar</td></tr>
</table>

LIST OF FIGURES

1. Problem Solving using Computers.. 1
Fig. 1.1: Recipe for making a cup of tea 3
Fig. 1.2: Classification of computational devices. 4
Fig. 1.3: Diagram of calculator 4
Fig. 1.4: A stored-program computer 4
Fig. 1.5: Simplified representation of computer memory 6
Fig. 1.6: Execution of a C program 9
Fig. 1.7: Snapshot of Code::blocks IDE for programming 11
Fig. 1.8: First program in C 11
Fig. 1.9: Program using minimum possible separators 13
Fig. 1.10: Program written with proper spacing 14
Fig. 1.11: Example of declaring and defining the variables 17
Fig. 1.12: Input/output in C 18

2. Operators and Input-Output in C.. 26
Fig. 2.1: Demonstration of arithmetic and assignment operators 30
Fig. 2.2: Demonstration of relational operators 31
Fig. 2.3: Demonstration of the logical AND operator 32
Fig. 2.4: Demonstration of the logical AND operator 32
Fig. 2.5: Demonstration of the logical OR operator 33
Fig. 2.6: Demonstration of the logical OR operator 33
Fig. 2.7: Demonstration of the logical NOT operator 34
Fig. 2.8: Demonstration of the bitwise operators 35
Fig. 2.9: Demonstration of the unary operators 37
Fig. 2.10: Demonstration of the increment and decrement unary operators 39
Fig. 2.11: Demonstration of the ternary operator 40
Fig. 2.12: Data types from top to bottom in increasing order of memory size. 41
Fig. 2.13: Demonstration of the implicit type conversion 41
Fig. 2.14: Demonstration of the explicit type conversion 42
Fig. 2.15: Precedence and the associativity of the operators 43
Fig. 2.16: Evaluation of x=2+3*4-7/2 43
Fig. 2.17: Evaluation of x=2+3*4-7/2<6<12 44
Fig. 2.18: Evaluation of x=2+3*4-7/2<6<12 && 10<71/6 45

Fig. 2.19: Demonstration the use of various integer and floating-point conversion specifiers 48
Fig. 2.20: Demonstration the use of string and character conversion specifier 49
Fig. 2.21: Demonstration the concept of field width 50
Fig. 2.22: Demonstration of the integer conversion specifiers 52
Fig. 2.23: Demonstration of the writing a file 54
Fig. 2.24: Demonstration of reading a file 54

3. Control Statements in C 62

Fig. 3.1: Flowchart of computing the average temperature of all the working days of a month 64
Fig. 3.2: Types of control statements 65
Fig. 3.3: Flowchart of if statement 66
Fig. 3.4: Demonstration of the if statement 66
Fig. 3.5: Interpretation of if statement 66
Fig. 3.6: Flowchart of if..else statement 67
Fig. 3.7: Demonstration of if..else statement 68
Fig. 3.8: Flowchart of if-else-if statement 69
Fig. 3.9: Demonstration of if-else-if statement 70
Fig. 3.10: Flowchart of nested if-else statement 71
Fig. 3.11: Demonstration of nested if-else statement 72
Fig. 3.12: Demonstration of dangling else 73
Fig. 3.13: Demonstration of dangling else 73
Fig. 3.14: Flowchart of the switch statement 73
Fig. 3.15: Demonstration of switch statement 75
Fig. 3.16: Flowchart to play song playlist 76
Fig. 3.17: Flowchart of while loop 76
Fig. 3.18: Program to print numbers from 0 to 4 using a while loop 77
Fig. 3.19: Flowchart of for loop 78
Fig. 3.20: Program to print numbers from 0 to 4 using a for loop 79
Fig. 3.21: Flowchart of the do-while loop 81
Fig. 3.22: Program to print numbers from 0 to 4 using a do-while loop 81
Fig. 3.23: Demonstration of the break statement 83
Fig. 3.24: Demonstration of the continue statement 83
Fig. 3.25: Example to check prime number 84
Fig. 3.26: Calculator using the do-while loop 85
Fig. 3.27: Flow chart of the nested loop 86

Fig. 3.28: Demonstration of the nested loop 87
Fig. 3.29: Program to calculate the factorial 88
Fig. 3.30: Demonstration of the goto statement 89
Fig. 3.31: Flowchart to check even or odd number 98

4. Arrays and Functions in C **99**
Fig. 4.1: Array Example 101
Fig. 4.2: Runtime initialization of an array 103
Fig. 4.3: Memory allocation and address representation in an array 103
Fig. 4.4: Memory layout 104
Fig. 4.5: Visualization and components of the stack 105
Fig. 4.6: Visualization of the variable and pointer 106
Fig. 4.7: Demonstration of the pointer 107
Fig. 4.8: Demonstration of the arithmetic operations in pointer 108
Fig. 4.9: Demonstration of different types of pointers 109
Fig. 4.10: Demonstration to read a string from the user 110
Fig. 4.11: Representation of 2-Dimensional Array (marks) 111
Fig. 4.12: Different ways to initialize a 2-D array 112
Fig. 4.13: 2-Dimensional array (marks) representation in a row and column-major order 113
Fig. 4.14: Types of function 114
Fig. 4.15: Demonstration of working of a smallest function 117
Fig. 4.16: Demonstration of working of a cube function 116
Fig. 4.17: Demonstration of call by value method of function calling 118
Fig. 4.18: Demonstration of call by reference method of function calling 120
Fig. 4.19: Program to calculate the length of the hypotenuse of a right-angled triangle 121
Fig. 4.20: Program to calculate the length of the hypotenuse of a right-angled triangle 122
Fig. 4.21: Demonstration of passing an array to functions 123
Fig. 4.22: Demonstration of use of the auto variable 124
Fig. 4.23: Demonstration of the use of extern variable 125
Fig. 4.24: Demonstration of the use of static variable 126
Fig. 4.25: Demonstration of use of the register variable 126

5. Recursion and Recursive Solutions **134**
Fig. 5.1: Iterative and Recursive way to find the car key 136
Fig. 5.2: Representation of the base and recursive case 136
Fig. 5.3: Demonstration of the recursive function 137

Fig. 5.4: Step-by-step working of the recursive function 138
Fig. 5.5: Demonstration of the tail recursion 138
Fig. 5.6: Demonstration of the head recursion 139
Fig. 5.7: Demonstration of the tree recursion 139
Fig. 5.8: Demonstration of the nested recursion 140
Fig. 5.9: Graphical representation of the indirect recursion 140
Fig. 5.10: Demonstration of the indirect recursion 141
Fig. 5.11: Tower of Hanoi 142
Fig. 5.12: Demonstration of the Tower of Hanoi 143
Fig. 5.13: Graphical representation of the binary search 144
Fig. 5.14: Demonstration of the Binary Search 145
Fig. 5.15: Demonstration of the command line arguments 151

LIST OF TABLES

1. Problem Solving using Computers **1**
Table 1.1: Lists of the keywords 13
Table 1.2: Memory required and ranges of various data types 15

2. Operators and Input-Output in C **26**
Table 2.1: Assignment operators in C language 29
Table 2.2: Different types of relational operators 30
Table 2.3: Basic bitwise operators 34
Table 2.4: Integer and Floating-point Conversion Specifiers 47
Table 2.5: Commonly used escape sequences 49
Table 2.6: The basic functions of handling a file in C 52

CONTENTS

Foreword *iii*
Acknowledgement *v*
Preface *vii*
Outcome Based Education *ix*
Course Outcomes *x*
Guidelines for Teachers *xi*
Guidelines for Students *xii*
Abbreviations and Symbols *xiii*
List of Figures *xiv*
List of Tables *xviii*

1. Problem Solving using Computers..1-25

Unit Specifics 1
Rationale 1
Pre-requisites 2
Unit Outcomes 2
1.1 Introduction 2
1.1.1 Computational Thinking and Problem Solving 3
1.2 Computing devices 4
1.2.1 Fixed Program Computers 4
1.2.2 Stored Program Computer 4
1.2.3 Computer Memory Representation 5
1.3 How to communicate with computers 6
1.3.1 Machine Language 6
1.3.2 Assembly Language 7
1.3.3 Natural Language 7
1.4 Programming Language 7
1.4.1 Types of Instructions 8
1.5 Introduction to C programming language 9
1.5.1 Execution of a C Program 9
1.5.2 Need of a Compiler 10
1.5.3 Different Available Compilers for C and the Integrated Development Environments (IDEs) 10
1.5.4 First Program in C 11

1.6 Basic elements of C language 12
1.6.1 Keywords 13
1.6.2 Identifiers 13
1.6.3 Separators 13
1.6.4 Constant, Data Types and Variables 14
1.6.5 Pre-define Function and Syntax 17
1.6.6 Operators 17
1.7 Input/output in C (Practice example) 17
Unit Summary 19
Exercises 20
Exercise 21
Practical 23
Know More 23
References and Suggested Readings 25

2. Operators and Input-Output in C 26-61
Unit Specifics 26
Rationale 26
Pre-requisites 26
Unit Outcomes 27
2.1 Expressions and Operators in C 27
2.2 Binary Operators 27
2.3 Unary Operator 36
2.4 Ternary Operator 40
2.5 Implicit and Explicit-type Conversions 40
2.5.1 Implicit Type Conversion 41
2.5.2 Explicit Type Conversion 42
2.6 Precedence and associativity of C operators 42
2.7 Input and Output in C Programming 45
2.7.1 Output with Printf Function 46
2.7.1.1 Printing Integers and Floating-point Numbers 46
2.7.1.2 Printing Strings and Characters 49
2.7.2 Escape Sequence 49
2.7.3 Field widths and Precision in Printf 50

2.8 Input Using Scanf Function 51

2.9 Input and Output from Files 52

2.9.1 What is a File? 52

2.9.2 File Operations 53

Unit Summary 55

Exercises 56

Practical 59

Know More 60

References and Suggested Readings 61

3. Control Statements in C 62-98

Unit Specifics 62

Rationale 62

Pre-requisites 62

Unit Outcomes 63

3.1 Introduction 63

3.2 Control Statements 64

3.3 Selection Statement 65

3.3.1 The if Statement 65

3.3.2 The if-else Statement 67

3.3.3 The if-else-if Statement 68

3.3.4 The Nested if-else Statement 70

3.3.5 The Switch Statement 74

3.4 Repetition Statement 75

3.4.1 Entry Control Loop 76

3.4.2 Exit Control Loop 80

3.4.3 Nested Loop 86

3.4.4 Goto Statement 88

Unit Summary 89

Exercises 91

Practical 96

Know More 97

References and Suggested Readings 98

4. Arrays and Functions in C **99-133**

Unit Specifics 99

Rationale 99

Pre-requisites 99

Unit Outcomes 100

4.1 Introduction 100

4.2 Array 101

4.2.1 Array Declaration and Initialization 101

4.3 Memory Organization in C 103

4.4 Pointers 106

4.4.1 Arithmetic Operation in Pointer 107

4.4.2 Types of Pointers 108

4.5 String as Array of Characters 109

4.5.1 Initialization of a String 109

4.5.2 Reading a String from User 110

4.6 Multidimensional Array 111

4.7 Function 113

4.7.1 Advantages of using Functions 114

4.7.2 Types of Functions 114

4.7.3 Function Definition, Declaration, and Calling 114

4.7.4 Function Calling 118

4.7.5 Passing Array to Functions 122

4.8 Storage Classes 124

Unit Summary 127

Exercises 129

Practical 132

Know More 133

References and Suggested Readings 133

5. Recursion and Recursive Solutions **134-151**

Unit Specifics 134

Rationale 134

Pre-requisites 135

Unit Outcomes 135

5.1 Introduction 135

5.2 Types of Recursions 138

5.2.1 Direct Recursion 138

5.2.2 Indirect Recursion 140

5.3 Recursive Solutions 141

5.3.1 Factorial 141

5.3.2 Towers of Hanoi 142

5.3.3 Binary Search 143

Unit Summary 146

Exercises 146

Practical 149

Know More 149

References and Suggested Readings 151

Appendices **153**

References For Further Learning **157**

CO and PO Attainment Table **159**

Index **161**

1 Problem Solving using Computers

UNIT SPECIFICS

Through this unit, we have discussed the following aspects:

- Basic knowledge of computers;
- Computational thinking and problem-solving;
- Aspects of the programming language;
- Giving instructions to a computer using a programming language;
- Introduction to C language and its component;
- Basic programming examples with explanation;

The topics are discussed with various examples for generating further curiosity and creativity and improving problem-solving capacity.

Besides giving a large number of multiple choice questions as well as questions of short and long answer types marked in two categories following lower and higher order of Bloom's taxonomy, assignments through several numerical problems, a list of references, and suggested readings are given in the unit so that one can go through them for practice. It is important to note that for getting more information on various topics of interest, some QR codes have been provided in different sections, which can be scanned for relevant supportive knowledge.

After the related practical, based on the content, there is a "Know More" section. This section has been carefully designed so that the supplementary information provided in this part becomes beneficial for the users of the book. This section mainly highlights the initial activity, examples of some interesting facts, analogy, history of the development of the subject focusing on the salient observations and finding, timelines starting from the development of the concerned topics up to the recent time, applications of the subject matter for our day-to-day real life or/and industrial applications on a variety of aspects, case study related to environmental, sustainability, social and ethical issues whichever applicable, and finally inquisitiveness and curiosity topics of the unit.

RATIONALE

This introductory unit on problem-solving through computers helps students to get a basic idea of problem-solving and computational thinking. It gives basic knowledge of a computer, its components from the programming perspective, and explains the idea of incorporating problem-solving skills in a computer through programming. Instead of directly going to the programming language, this chapter clarifies to the reader the need for a programming language to solve a computational problem using computers. It explains the various aspects of a programming language with examples. Next, it covers the introduction of the C language and its features. Though this book will use the C language for computer programming, most of the fundamental part covered in this unit is applicable to all programming languages.

Computer programming is the core subject in the computer science field. Using any computer programming, one can solve computational problems using computers. Moreover, all the software and applications are built using various programming languages. The practical applications of this book cover, all the computational devices, software, web applications etc. that one interact with in the daily life.

PRE-REQUISITES

Basic Mathematics

UNIT OUTCOMES

List of outcomes of this unit is as follows:

U1-O1: Describe the problem solving and computational thinking

U1-O2: Describe the basic knowledge of a computer and its component

U1-O3: Explain various aspects of a programming language

U1-O4: Realize the role of computer programming in solving real-world problems

U1-O5: Understand C programming fundamentals

Unit-1 Outcomes	EXPECTED MAPPING WITH COURSE OUTCOMES (1- Weak Correlation; 2- Medium correlation; 3- Strong Correlation)					
	CO-1	CO-2	CO-3	CO-4	CO-5	CO-6
U1-O1	2	3	2	-	-	-
U1-O2	3	2	2	2	-	-
U1-O3	2	2	3	-	-	-
U1-O4	2	3	3	1	-	-
U1-O5	2	2	2	3	-	-

1.1 INTRODUCTION

Now computers are everywhere. Here, a computer is not only referred to as a Laptop or Desktop but any device that performs some computation. Any computing device does two main tasks: performing computation and remembering the computation results. The typical computer sitting on a table or a desk performs a billion calculations in a second. We utilize them to do multiple tasks speedily and more accurately. For instance, we can reserve train tickets online using a computer or smartphone.

For most of human history, the computation was constrained by the speed of calculation of the human brain and the capability of manually recording the results of computations. We hope that by reading this book, you will feel comfortable using computational thinking to solve many of the problems you come across during studies, work, and in institutes. The term "computerization" typically refers to the effective use of computers to create software that automates any repetitive human work. Computers are used to solve various problems; therefore, one of the essential skills a computer science student should possess is problem-solving. It is important to note that computers cannot solve problems independently. We must provide clear, step-by-step directions on how to solve a given problem. The effectiveness of a computer in solving a problem depends on how exactly and correctly the problem is defined, the algorithm is created to resolve it, and then implements the algorithm by a programming language. Thus, problem-solving is the process of recognizing a problem, creating an algorithm to solve it, and then implementing it using a programming language.

1.1.1 Computational Thinking and Problem Solving

Before diving into the problem-solving process using a programming language (in this book, we will follow the C language), let us first understand computational thinking. The knowledge can be divided into two parts: Declarative knowledge and Imperative knowledge.

A. Declarative knowledge: Declarative knowledge refers to statements that are fact. For example, 2, 4, and 6 are even numbers. Similarly, 3, 5, and 7 are odd numbers. Though, these statements are facts and contain some knowledge. But still, it does not tell us how we can check if an arbitrary number is odd or even.

B. Imperative knowledge: It is something like an instruction (or set of instructions), or informally, we can call a *recipe* that gives the information about how to do certain things. For example, informally, we can check if a number is odd or even by performing the following steps.

- Take an arbitrary number, let's say *n*.
- Divide the number n by *two* and observe the remainder, let's say *r*.
- If *r* is equal to 0, then we can say the number is even.
- Otherwise, if *r* is a non-zero value, then the number is odd.

By performing the above step-by-step instructions, we can check whether any number is even or odd. This type of knowledge is called imperative knowledge, and in computer science, this step-by-step description is called an **Algorithm** (or *pseudocode*). It is like a recipe from a cookbook such that you will eventually get the desired result if performed correctly.

Another real-world example of a recipe for making a cup of tea is given in Fig.1.1.

```
1.  Place water in a Tea-Pot
2.  Boil the water
3.  Put tea leaves in Tea-Pot
4.  Add milk into the Tea-Pot
5.  Add some sugar cubes
6.  Boil for some time
7.  Pour the tea into a cup using a tea strainer
```

Fig.1.1: Recipe for making a cup of tea

Question 1.1 *How can we give this task (set of instructions) to a computing device?*

1.2 COMPUTING DEVICES

There are two ways to perform a task from a computing device. One is to develop the machine hardware in such a way that it will perform the specific task - Fixed program computers. In another way, instead of fixing instructions during the machine hardware development, the computing device takes these instructions from users/operators and performs the given task based on the instructions given - Stored program computers.

Scan QR code for details

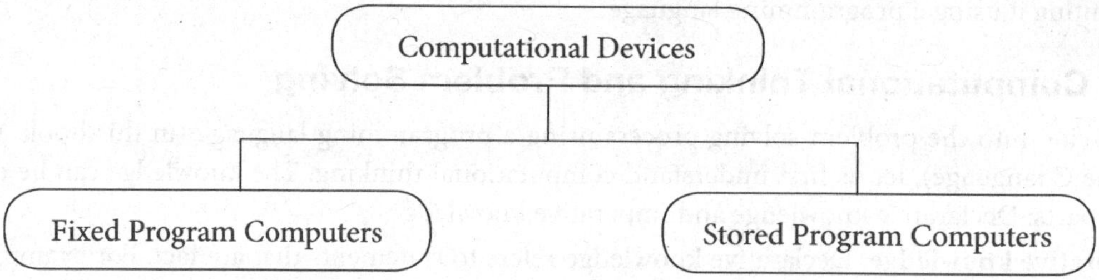

Fig.1.2: Classification of computational devices.

1.2.1 Fixed Program Computers

When a computing device performs only a specific task, i.e., it cannot be programmed for other tasks. For example, a calculator can only perform the arithmetic or logic operations available. You give the numbers as the input, and when you press '+' it performs addition. Similarly, all the operations available can be performed. However, you cannot perform any other computation which is not available in the calculator.

Fig.1.3: Diagram of calculator

1.2.2 Stored Program Computer

In a stored program concept, the computer performs the task stored or given to the computer. Modern computers are based on this concept. The simplest block diagram of a Stored programmed computer is shown in Figure 1.4. It contains three fundamental components.

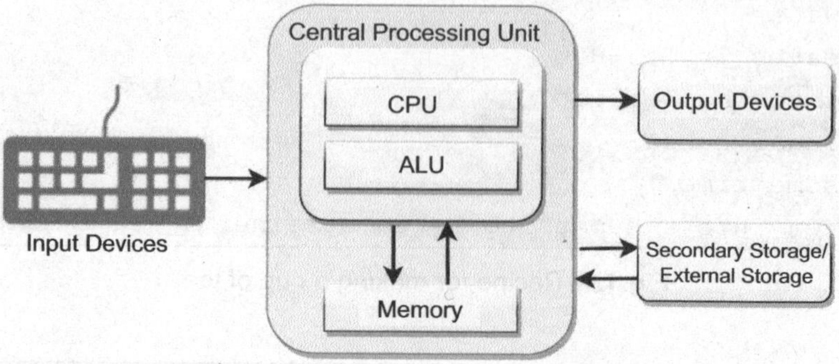

Fig.1.4: A stored-program computer

A. Central Processing Unit (CPU): It is the brain of the computer which executes the programs. It plays a crucial role in program executions without which the program cannot be run. We can say that a program is executed when the CPU performs the instructions received from the program.

B. Memory: Memory can be viewed as the computer's workspace where the computer stores the program/application and data required for execution. For instance, writing an essay using a word application. During the execution of that task, both essay and word processing applications will be stored in the memory.

C. Input/Output: Input is data that a computer receives from another device or any user through an input device. Input devices are the components that gather the data and send it to the computers. So, a device that gives the input to the computer is called the input device. For example, keyboard, QR code scanner, mouse, etc. The optical and disk drives are also referred to as input devices because the program and required data are loaded into the main memory.

Output is the data produced by the computer for the user or other devices. Output data can be a list of the names, graphic images, and results of a computation. The output data is sent through the output devices. It sends the data from the computer to another computer or user. Basic output devices are monitors, printers, etc. CD recorders and disk drives are the output devices as they store the output data sent by the computer.

The CPU is intended to perform operations like:

```
1. Reading the data from the memory.
2. Subtracting one number from another number
3. Adding two numbers
4. Dividing one number by another number
5. Multiplying two numbers
6. Calculating a value is equivalent to another value
7. Moving data across memory locations
```

The above list demonstrates that the CPU only handles basic data operations. However, the CPU does not act on its own. The goal of a program is to instruct the CPU on what to do. The CPU performs operations as a result of this list of instructions. These step-to-step instructions, written in any programming language, are also known as a **Program or Application.**

The data (input/output) associated with every computation problem can be of any type such as numbers, characters, or words (strings). Further, numbers can be of different types, such as integers like 0, 1, 2, 3, -1, -2, etc., and fractional values 1.2, 0.6, and so on. Before study that how to use different types of data in C. Let us first understand how data is stored in the computer.

1.2.3 Computer Memory Representation

As we know, computers work on binary data representation (0s and 1s). The computer's memory is split into tiny units called bytes. A single letter or small number is stored in a single byte. To perform the tasks, the computer has lots of sequences of bytes. The majority of modern computers have billions of bytes of memory.

Each byte of memory can be identified by a unique address. It is similar to the address of a house in the real world. Houses have unique addresses associated with them. Different types of data require different memory sizes. A simplified representation of computer memory is shown in Figure 1.5.

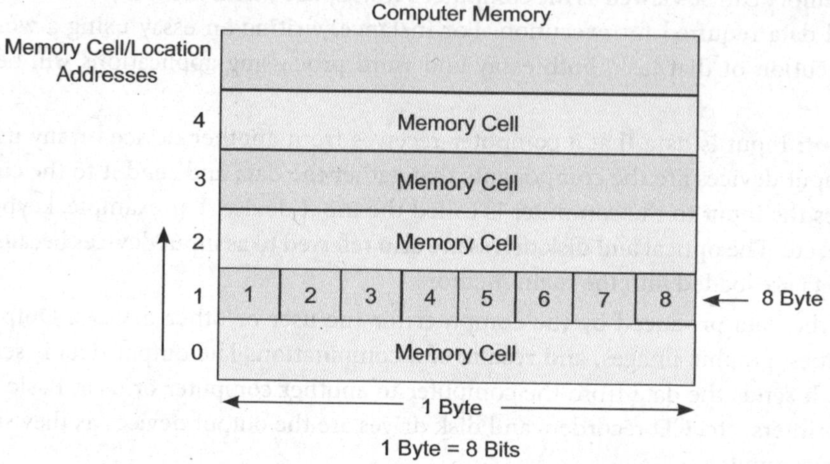

Scan QR code for video lecture

Fig.1.5: Simplified representation of computer memory

The next question is how to write this step-to-step program or communicate with computers.

Question 1.2: How to communicate set of instructions with a computer?

1.3 HOW TO COMMUNICATE WITH COMPUTERS

Now, the question is how to give a task (set of instructions) to the computer. Here, there are two aspects: hardware view and software view. From a hardware perspective, we give the task through input devices. From a software perspective, we have to give a task in a language that the computer understands. We are going to emphasize the latter perspective. First, we must understand how computers understand instructions and how humans communicate.

1.3.1 Machine Language

The computer architecture comprises several billion transistors turned on by the electronic signals it receives. A transistor's on and off states are represented by the binary digits 1 and 0, respectively. Only binary-coded instructions are understood and carried out by the computer. It is unable to carry out any instructions given in a different format. As a result, we must provide the computer instructions in binary. Therefore, all our computer programs must be written in a binary language (series of 0s and 1s).

A program's instructions direct the CPU to carry out particular actions. Here is an illustration of a command that might be present in a program:

```
10110000
```

This is just a string of 1s and 0s to a user. However, to a CPU, it is an instruction to operate. This is a genuine **Intel microprocessor** instruction. It instructs the CPU to move a value into the microprocessor. However, this is an operating instruction to a CPU.

1.3.2 Assembly Language

It is not practical for individuals to develop a program in machine language, even though a computer's CPU can only understand it. As a substitute for machine language, assembly language was developed in the earlier days of computing. Assembly language employs mnemonics, or short words, in place of binary numbers to represent instructions. For instance, the mnemonics *add, mul*, and *mov* in assembly language often refers to adding, multiplying, and transferring values to different locations in memory, respectively.

However, the CPU cannot run assembly language programs. An assembly language program is converted to a machine language program using a specialized program called an **assembler**. Assembly language is usually used as a replacement for a machine language. However, Assembly language still has some drawbacks. It necessitates extensive knowledge of the CPU like a machine language. Even the most straightforward program written in assembly language requires you to write numerous instructions. Assembly language is also known as a low-level language as it is similar to machine language.

1.3.3 Natural Language

However, even with assembly language, it is not easy for humans to write every program in assembly language. While computers can only process binary language, humans are proficient at conveying instructions in English. Humans understand and communicate in natural languages like English, Hindi, Tamil, etc. However, Human understandable languages are **ambiguous**. For, e.g., the sentence "I saw a girl on the hill with a telescope" is ambiguous. The sentence can be interpreted as either seeing a girl with a telescope on the hill or seeing a girl holding a telescope.

In summary, there are three requirements for a high-level language to communicate with computers

1. Similar to human-like (natural) language: *for ease of use*
2. Unambiguous in nature: *only a single meaning of an instruction*
3. Mediator (A Program/Application): *that can convert the language into an understandable computer format.*

Therefore, there is a need for a programming language similar to an English-like language, has a single meaning for each instruction, and can be converted into computer machine language. A detailed description of programming languages is given in the next section.

1.4 Programming Language

Various programming languages fulfill the above three requirements to communicate with computers like C, C++, Java, Python, and so on. There is no ideal language (although some could be considered the worst). For various applications, different languages work better or worse. For example, MATLAB is a great language for working with matrices and vectors. Programs that manage data networks can be written effectively in C. For creating websites, PHP is an impactful language. Furthermore, Python is a useful general-purpose language. This book focuses on the C language to understand all the programming concepts. There are three aspects of any programming language.

1. **Syntax:** Syntax determines whether combinations of symbols and characters are well-formed or not in any language. For instance, the sentence "*run swim fly*" is not syntactically correct. The English language does not support syntax in the form of `<verb><verb><verb>`. Similarly, in the C language, the primitives +10 20 are not in the valid sequence; however, 10+20 is the valid sequence.

2. **Statics Semantic:** The static semantics are responsible for checking whether a string is valid based on the syntactically or not. For example, "We am friends" is in the form of `<noun><verb><adjective>`, is a syntactically correct sentence, but it is not a correct English sentence. Because "*We*" is plural and the verb "am" is singular. This kind of error is known as static semantic error. In the C programming language, 2.34*'x' is syntactically correct but gives a static semantic error because the fractional value cannot be multiplied by the character.
3. **Semantic:** The semantics of a language associates a meaning with each syntactically correct string of symbols with no static semantic errors. The meaning of the sentence may be hazy or unclear in natural languages. For instance, the sentence "call me a taxi, please" can be either a person's name is a taxi, or he wants to go somewhere by taxi. For the smooth functioning computer needs proper and clear instructions, that's why programming languages ensure that each program has only one meaning.

With any programming language, syntax errors are most likely to occur. However, it is easy to handle because all the programming languages (their compilers) detect the syntax errors and report them to the programmers. Semantic errors are hard to handle because programming language does not indicate them. It is mostly due to bad logic/operations the programmer writes. So, finding and fixing them is the programmer's responsibility.

1.4.1 Types of Instructions

Normally, the CPU executes instructions (written in any programming language) one by one in a sequential manner. This is called the flow of execution (or flow of control). However, concerning a particular problem, the control flow might change. For example, see the example of identifying odd and even numbers (reiterating the example given in Section 1.2).

```
1. Take an arbitrary number, let's say n.
2. Divide the number n by two and observe the remainder, let's say r.
3. If r is equal to 0, then we can say the number is even.
4. Otherwise, the number is odd if r is a non-zero value.
```

In this example, the CPU will start the execution from step 1. With the normal flow of control, it will go to step 2. However, if you see the example, the execution of step 3 (or 4) depends on the result of step 2 and only one step (3 or 4) will be executed. Moreover, some instructions might need to be executed more than once, for example, adding a number 100 times.

Therefore all the programming languages provide different types of instructions for various tasks. In C language, all these instructions can be divided into three types.

1. **Type Declaration Instruction:** These instructions are used to declare required variables in the C program.
2. **Arithmetic Instruction:** These instructions are used to perform arithmetic operations in C programming.
3. **Control Instruction:** These types of instruction are used to control the flow and execution sequence of the statements in the c program.

In the following sections, we will see the C language constructs, features, data types, and instructions that can be used to solve a problem.

1.5 INTRODUCTION TO C PROGRAMMING LANGUAGE

C programming is a high-level and general-purpose computer programming language developed by Dennis Ritchie in 1972. It was primarily developed as a system programming language to write operating systems. The C language's primary characteristics are low-level memory access, a limited set of keywords, and a clean style, which make it appropriate for system programs like operating systems or compiler development. Also, the C programming language is case-sensitive, which means that capital and small alphabets have distinct meanings.

1.5.1 Execution of a C Program

This section describes the execution of a C program. A file with the extension '*.c*' is a source file. When the compiler compiles the source file, then at each step, it creates a new file. These new files have the same name as the source file but have a different extension. The complete execution of a C program is shown in Figure 1.6.

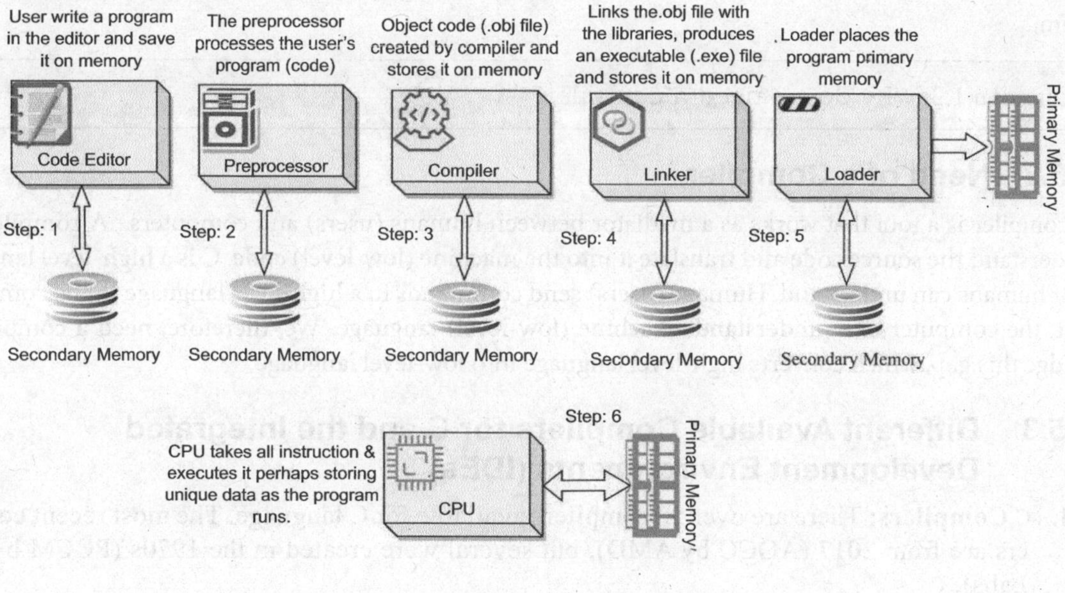

Fig.1.6: Execution of a C program

Code Editor: This is the first step of writing a program. We require an editor/IDE where the source code of a program can be written and saved with a *.c* extension. The .c extension helps the compiler to recognize a C program file. Let us say there is a C program file called *FirstProgram.c.* It is the source file containing the program's code.

Preprocessor: Preprocessor takes source code (*FirstProgram.c*) as input and eliminates the comments, expands the include file and macros, etc. The preprocessed file is stored with the *.i* (*FirstProgram.i*) extension and send to the compiler.

Compiler: In this step, the compiler checks the errors in the code (*FirstProgram.i*). If there are no errors, the C compiler saves it with the *.obj* extension as an object file. As a result, *FirstProgram.obj* will be created. This *.obj* file cannot be executed. The Linker continues the process, producing an executable file with the .exe extension.

Linker: Let us start by clarifying that library functions are a component of C software, not any specific C program. As a result, the compiler is unaware of how any function, including *printf* and *scanf*, actually works. These functions' definitions are kept in the corresponding libraries, which must be linked. The Linker reads #include a keyword, it links the header file, written inside the triangular bracket (*<stdio.h>*) with the objective file. The header files provide access to the input/output function like *printf, scanf, etc.* Once the linker links all the library functions with the objective file, the program will be converted into the *.exe* file. Hence, the executable file *firstProgram.exe* will be generated.

Loader: The loader works whenever we instruct a specific application to execute. The loader loads the given .exe (*FirstProgram.exe*) file in the RAM. After loading, the file loader will update the program's starting address and inform the CPU.

CPU: In this step, the CPU takes all the instructions from the loaded executable file and executes them.

Question 1.3: why do we need a compiler?

1.5.2 Need of a Compiler

A compiler is a tool that works as a mediator between humans (users) and computers. A compiler can understand the source code and translate it into the machine (low-level) code. C is a high-level language that humans can understand. Humans (users) send commands in a high-level language to the computer. But, the computer only understands machine (low-level) language. We, therefore, need a compiler to bridge this gap, which converts high-level language into low-level language.

1.5.3 Different Available Compilers for C and the Integrated Development Environments (IDEs)

1. **C Compilers:** There are over 50 compilers available for C language. The most recent compilers are from 2017 (AOCC by AMD), but several were created in the 1970s (PCCM by Bell Labs).

   Different compilers are required to optimize the compiled C code for particular hardware and software environments. For instance, AOCC is optimized for AMD systems, while ICC by Intel is optimized for Intel systems. Similar to this, other compilers focus on various operating systems. *Acorn C, Clang, MSVC, Open64, TCC, gcc, and MinGW* are a few of the available compilers.

2. **IDEs:** IDE is an application that facilitates the development of other applications. They are typically designed to facilitate the work of developers and enhance their output by offering a variety of practical features, including code editors, debugging assistance, compilers, auto code completion, and many more. There are numerous C and *C++ IDEs* available to do programming without hassle. Some of them are *Visual Studio, Eclipse, Dev C++, Xcode, Code::Blocks, Turbo C, CodeLite, NetBeans* etc.

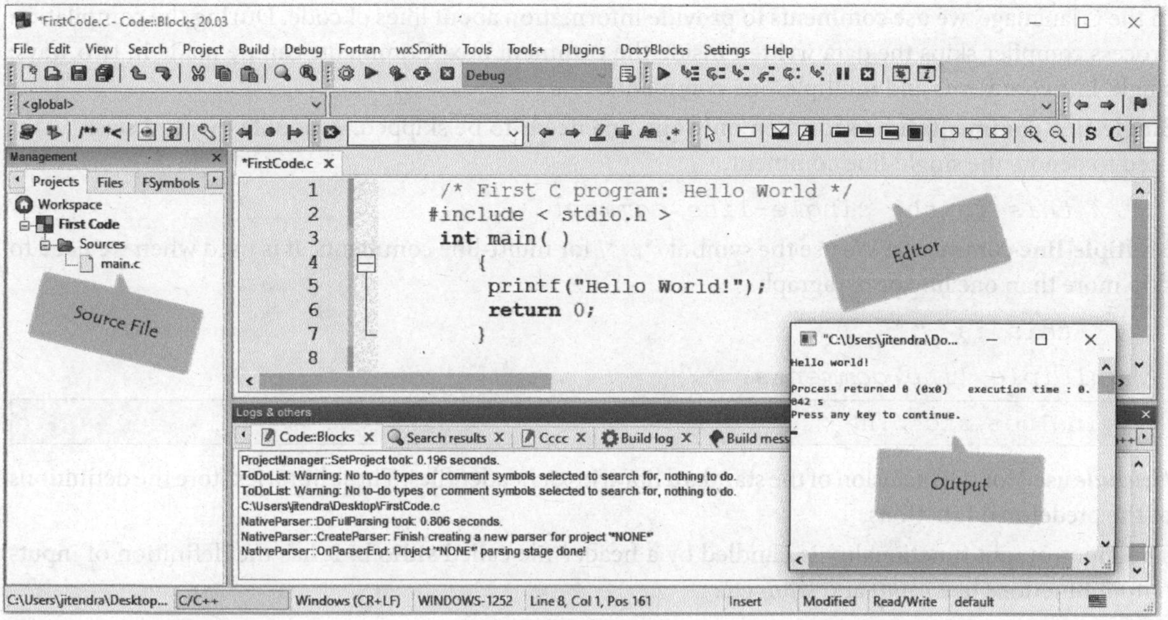

Fig.1.7: Snapshot of Code::blocks IDE for programming

1.5.4 First Program in C

A programming language can only be learned by writing programs in it. The first program in the C language is:

```
/* First C program: Hello programmers!*/
#include<stdio.h>
int main()
{
 printf("Hello programmers!");
 return 0;
}
```

Fig.1.8: First program in C

Explanation:

```
/* First C program: Hello programmers!*/
```

In the C language, we use comments to provide information about lines of code. During the compilation process compiler skips the data written inside the comment box. Comments can be made in two ways: single-line comments and multiple-line comments.

Single-line comments are used when only one line needs to be skipped. A double forward slash (//) is used to denote the single-line comment.

```
// this is the single-line comment.
```

Multiple-line comments: We use the symbol /*... */ for multi-line comments. It is used when we need to skip more than one line or paragraph.

```
/* this is
multiple line comments. */
```

```
#include<stdio.h>
```

#include used for the inclusion of the standard libraries or header files. These libraries store the definitions of the predefined functions.

The input-output functionality is handled by a header file called **stdio.h**. It has the definition of input-output functions like *printf* and *scanf* etc.

```
int main()
```

The main function serves as the entry point for all C programs. All the instructions should be written or referred to inside the *main( )* function.

```
{
   //instructions
   return 0;
}
```

The braces {and} specify the function block's scope. After the execution of the function program will return to the called place with the returned value. In terms of the *main( )* function, the program finishes the execution and returns to the environment where the program was executing. The *main()* function returns an integer representing the program's exit status, where 0 represents the successful exit.

```
printf("Hello programmers!");
```

In the above line, there is only one statement in this program: *printf ()*. The *printf()* function is predefined in *stdio.h* header file, which displays the characters written inside the double quote (" ") on the output screen (Monitor).

1.6 BASIC ELEMENTS OF C LANGUAGE

C programming language has the following important elements:

1. Keywords
2. Identifiers
3. Separators
4. Constants, Data Types and Variables
5. Pre-define functions and Syntax
6. Operators

1.6.1 Keywords

Every language has certain words that can be used to construct a statement. The C programming language supports some words with their specific meanings, which are used to construct the c programming statements or instructions. These special words are referred to as reserved words or keywords. The C programming language has 32 keywords, as shown in Table 1.1. Each of the 32 keywords has been pre-defined, and the compiler already knows their meaning.

Table 1.1: Lists of the keywords

if	else	double	int	float	struct	break	auto
long	switch	case	enum	register	typedef	char	extern
return	union	const	short	unsigned	continue	for	signed
void	default	goto	sizeof	volatile	do	static	while

1.6.2 Identifiers

The identifier is the name or identity used to recognize the variables, functions, etc. Identifiers are created by combining the alphabets underscore (_) and digits. It is case-sensitive, which means uppercase and lowercase alphabets have distinct meanings. The identifier's first letter must be an underscore or an alphabet. The pre-defined or reserved words cannot be used as identifiers (e.g., *float, int, for*, etc.).

1.6.3 Separators

Separators are used to separate one programming component or element from one another. For instance, separating identifiers from identifiers, keywords from keywords, one identifier from another, etc. They resemble the punctuation marks used in English paragraphs.

Every word is separated by the white space, whereas statements are separated using semicolons (;) in C programming. There is a total of 14 separators supported by C programming. For Example: **, ; : ' ' " " { }** ***space*** etc.

Note: If the proper separators are used, the entire C program can be written in just two lines. The example is shown in Fig. 1.9.

```
#include <stdio.h>
int main(){printf(" Hello programmers!"); return 0;}
```

Fig.1.9: Program using minimum possible separators

The program in the above example (Fig.1.9) uses the minimum possible separators to display the message "`Hello programmers!`". Nevertheless, it is less readable and regarded as a bad programming practice. We should include suitable separators (indentation and spaces) to make a program understandable.

Think about the same program written correctly with separators that is much easier to read than the previous version (Figure 1.10).

```
#include<stdio.h>
int main()
{
    printf("Hello programmers!");
    return 0;
}
```

Fig.1.10: Program written with proper spacing

1.6.4 Constant, Data Types and Variables

A constant is a value or variable that remains unchanged throughout the entirety of the program. For example: 5, 25, 10, 'A', etc. In C language, constants are categorized into two types:

- Alphanumeric constants
- Numeric constants

1. **Alphanumeric Constant:** We can represent alphabets and 0–9 numbers using this constant. Alphanumeric constants are further classified into two types:
   - Character constant
   - String constant

   Any data represented in a single quote are called a character constant for example 'A', 'H', 'x', 'm', '#', '7', etc.

   The data represented within the double quotes are called a string constant for example, "Delhi", "programming", etc. The total number of characters in a C programming language is 256.
2. **Numeric Constant:** Numerical constants can be used to represent value-type data. The two types of numerical constants are integer and float.

   Representing a numeric value without any fractional part is called an integer. For example, 13, -13, 28, 54, -1248, and the representation of a numeric value with a fractional part is called float.

   For example 12.45, -34.12, 1.723.
3. **Data Types:** In the C programming language, data types assign memory to the variables. Every data type has its size in the form of the amount of memory. Based on the data types, specific amounts of memory and operations are assigned to the variables. Here are some basic data types:

char:	It is used to store one character. In most compilers, the memory requirement for char is one byte.
int:	It is used to store integer types of data.

float:	It is used to store fractional numbers.
void:	It shows no data types. It means no value. Functions that return nothing are usually specified using void data type.

Every data type has a different memory requirement. Based on the amount of memory, every data types have a specific range to store numbers. A list of data types with the amount of memory and their ranges is given in Table 1.2.

Table 1.2: Memory required and ranges of various data types

Data Type	Format Specifier	No of Bytes	Range
char (signed)	%c	1	128 to 127
unsigned char	%c	1	0 to 255
int (signed)	%d	2 or 4	-32768 to 32767
unsigned int	%u	2 or 4	0 to 65535
short int (signed)	%d	1	-128 to 127
unsigned short int	%u	1	0 to 255
long int (signed)	%ld	4	-2147483648 to 2147483647
unsigned long int	%lu	4	0 to 4294967295
float	%f	4	3.4E-38 to 3.4E+38
double	%lf	8	1.7E-308 to 1.7E+308

4. **Variables**: In simple terms, a variable is a place with some memory used to store different kinds of data. Each type of data requires a different size of memory. The type of variable is decided based on the type of data. The type also determines the range of values that can be kept in that memory and the range of operations a variable can perform.

   A variable name can be the combination of the alphabets, underscore, and digits, but it must begin with either underscore or alphabet. C language is case-sensitive; upper and lowercase alphabets will be distinct.
5. **Variable Definition in C**: When a variable is defined, the compiler is informed of where and how much storage should be allocated. The data type followed by names of one or more variables of the same type makes up a variable definition. The variable declaration has the following syntax:

type *list_of_variables;*

Here, type represents the data type; for example, *int, float, char*, etc. *list_of_variables* is the name of the variables; it can be a single variable or a list of multiple variables separated by the comma. Some of the valid variable declarations are as follows:

```
int l, m, n;
float p, q, r, s;
double i, j;
char x;
```

The line *int l, m, n;* declares and defines the variables and tells the compiler to create *int*-type variables *l, m, and n*. The compiler creates variables *l, m, and n* as integer types and stores integer data. Similarly, line ***float p, q, r, s;*** declares and defines four variables *p, q, r*, and *s* of float type. Line ***double i, j;*** declares and defines two variables *i* and *j* of double types, and line ***char x;*** declares and defines one variable *x* of character type.

The variables are initialized using the assignment operator (=) at the time of variable declaration. The syntax of the variable initialization is as follows:

type name_of_variable = value;

Some of the examples are as follows:

```
int n=10, m=20;           //defining and initializing n and m.
float p=0.5, q=1.141;     // defining and initializing p and q.
char var= 'h'             // The variable var holds the value 'h'. A
                             single quote ('') is used for a character
```

Variable Naming Rules: The name of a variable can be a single alphabet (like *a* and *b*) or in a descriptive form (like *marks, student_name, salary,* etc.).

The variable naming rules are as follows:

- A variable name can be started with the underscore (_) or the alphabet.
- A variable name cannot be started with the digit.
- A variable name can have a combination of alphabets (in upper and lower case), digits, and underscores.
- A variable name is case sensitive (marks and Marks are both treated as different variables).
- A variable name cannot contain any space.
- There is no limit on the length of the variable name.
- The variable name cannot be the keywords.

Some valid examples of the variable names are x, age, first_name, _amount, marks1, a2b, _xyz.

Invalid examples: 1x, first name, a-b.

Variable Declaration in C: The declaration of a variable assures the compiler that a variable with the specified type and name exists. The variable declaration allows the compiler to proceed further with the available information. In C language, all the variables must be declared before their use. A variable definition only has its meaning at the compilation time; the compiler requires the actual variable definition when linking the program. An example of variable declaration and definition is given in Figure 1.11.

Difference b/w Variable Declaration and Definition: When a variable is first introduced or declared before it is used, referred to as variable declaration. A variable definition refers to allocating the memory and value for a variable. The variable declaration and definition are generally made together.

```
#include<stdio.h>
int main()
{
    char x12 = 'H';     // declaration and definition of variable 'x12'
```

```
    float y;    // This is also both declaration and definition as 'y'
                // is allocated memory and assigned some garbage value.
    int _z, _xy73, v; // multiple declarations and definitions
    printf("%c", x12);  // printing the value of the variable

    return 0;
}
```

Fig.1.11: Example of declaring and defining the variables

1.6.5 Pre-define Function and Syntax

These are the set of pre-implemented functions available along with the compiler. They are used to perform any specific task.

Ex. *printf(), scanf(), strcpy(),* etc.

Syntax: The basic syntax of C language is every statement should end with a semicolon (;).

1.6.6 Operators

A special kind of symbol performs a specific task. There are 44 operators available in C programming language.

Ex. +, -, / %, etc.

1.7 Input/output in C (Practice example)

The program reads user input from the keyboard, calculates the result, and displays the output on the monitor. The standard library function *scanf* is utilized to fetch two numbers entered by the user at the keyboard. The program is shown in Fig.1.12.

```
#include<stdio.h>
/* Program execution start from the main function */
 int main()
{
    int number1;     /* variable number1 defined as an integer*/
    int number2;     /* variable number2 defined as an integer*/
    int result;    /* variable result stores addition of first and
                         second number  */
    printf("Enter first number \n");
    scanf("%d", &number1); /* reads first number inputted by user*/
printf("Enter second number \n" );
scanf("%d", &number2);    /* reads second number inputted by
                           user */
```

```
12. result= number1 + number2 ;   /*assignment of addition of number1
                                    and number2 to result*/
13. printf( "Addition is %d\n", result);    /* print result*/
14. return 0; /*indicates the successful execution of the
                  program */
15. } /*termination of the main function    */
```

Fig.1.12: Input/output in C

The program execution begins from the main function. The left brace { (line 4) marks the beginning of the main function's scope, which ends at the right brace } (line 15). Lines 5-7 define the variable definitions. The names number1, number2, and result are the identifier (name) of variables. A variable is a place in memory that can be used to hold a value for a program. The variables number1, number2, and result are all of the type int, which holds integer values. The variables must be defined with the data type followed by its name directly after the right brace that starts the main's body. The variable definition (lines 5-7) can be combined into a single statement, as seen below:

```
int number1, number2, result;
```

If we place the definition directly after the first *printf* statement, then it would cause a syntax error. When the compiler does not recognize a statement, a syntax error occurs. The compiler generates an error message and the line number to resolve the erroneous statements. These kinds of errors are generated by violating the language rules. These are also called compile-time errors. Line 8 displays the message Enter first number on the monitor.

```
printf("Enter first number \n");
```

The next line 9 uses the *scanf* statement to take input from the user. The function scanf reads the input from the input device (keyboard). The *scanf* function has two parameters, "*%d*" and "`&number1`".

```
scanf("%d", &number1);   /* reads first number inputted by user */
```

The format specifier, the first parameter outlines the type of data that the user should enter. The "%d" specifies that the data should be an integer. The second parameter begins with the address operator, ampersand (&), followed by the variable name i.e., &number1 defines the address in memory where the number1 (variable) should be stored. The variable number1's value is then kept in that memory address by the computer. Lines 10 display a message to enter the second number, and the cursor is moved to the start of the subsequent line, takes the value for the variable number2 from the user, and stores it at a memory location. Line 12 computes the total number1 and number2 of variables, and an assignment operator assigns the value to the variable result.

```
result = number1 + number2 ;   /*assignment of addition of number1 and
                                 number2 to result */
```

The + operator and assignment (=) operator are called as binary operator as these takes two operands to operate. The number1 and number2 are the operands of + operator. The result and expression value number1 + *number2* are the operands of = *operator.* An assignment operator assigns the value of the right hand's operand to the left hand's operand. Line 13 calls function *printf* to display the message written inside it.

```
printf( "Addition is %d\n", result);    /* print result */
```

There are two input parameters for function *printf*, "Addition is *%d\n*" and result. The first parameter is the format control string. It displays some messages and contains the format specifier *%d* indicates the printing of an integer. The value to be printed is specified by the second parameter. Additionally, calculations can be made inside *printf* statements. The two previous statements may have been combined into one statement.

```
printf(" Addition is %d \n ", number1 + number2);    /* print sum of
                                          number1 and number2  */
```

Line 14 indicates the program has been executed successfully. At line 15, the right brace signifies that the function main has ended.

In this unit, we studied the introduction of the C language characteristics and basic structure. In the remaining book, we will cover each of the expressions and types of instructions with their *syntax*, semantics, and usages.

UNIT SUMMARY

Section 1.1 Introduction

- **Computing device.** Any computing device (computer) does two main tasks: performing computation and remembering the computation results.
- **Problem-solving.** Problem-solving is recognizing a problem, creating a (step-by-step instructions) algorithm to solve it, and then implementing it to create a computer program.
- **Computational Thinking**
    - o **Declarative knowledge.** Statements that are fact. For example, 2, 4, and 6 are even numbers.
    - o **Imperative knowledge.** A set of instructions gives the information about how to do certain things.

Section 1.2 Computers

- **Types of Computers**
    - o **Fixed programmed computer**. A computing device performs only a specific task, i.e., it cannot be programmed for other tasks, e.g., Calculator.
    - o **Stored programmed computer.** In a stored program concept, the computer performs the task stored or given to the computer. All the stored programmed computer comprises of CPU, Memory, and Input/output devices.
    - o **Computer memory organization.** The memory of the computer is split into very small units that are called bytes. A single letter or small number is stored in a single byte. Each byte of memory can be identified by a unique address.

Section 1.3 How to communicate with computers

We have to give a task (instructions) in a language the computer understands. The computer understands binary language 0s and 1s.

- **Machine language.** The computer architecture comprises several billion transistors turned on by the electronic signals it receives (0 represents OFF (low voltage) and 1 ON (high voltage)). Therefore, computers understand the program written in a binary language (series of 0s and 1s).
- **Assembly language.** Assembly language employs mnemonics, or short words, in place of binary numbers to represent instructions. For instance, the mnemonics *add, mul, mov etc*. The **assembler** converts the assembly language to machine language.
- **Natural language.** Human understandable languages such as English, Hindi, Tamil, and so on. However, these are ambiguous in nature and cannot be used as a high-level programming language.

EXERCISES

Fill in the blanks

For the following statements, fill in the blanks:

1. In this unit, we discussed three types of languages: ___________, ___________ and ___________.
2. ___________ translates high-level language into machine language.
3. ___________ are generally used to write a program.
4. In C language, to read data from keyboard ___________ function is used.
5. The header file ___________ is included in the program for *printf, scanf* functions.

Answers:

1. machine languages, assembly languages and high-level languages.
2. Compiler
3. Editors/IDEs
4. Printf
5. stdio.h

EXERCISE

Multiple Choice Questions

1. Among the options below, which one is not a programming language?
   (a) c# (b) Java
   (c) C (d) Window
2. What is the function of a compiler?
   (a) Converting pseudo code to a computer program
   (b) Converting high-level language to machine-level language
   (c) Converting high-level program to binary digits
   (d) Converting integer to assembly language
3. The main components of CPU are:
   (a) Registers, ALU, Monitor (b) Control Unit, ALU, Hard Disk
   (c) Control Unit, ALU (d) Main Memory, ALU, Control Unit
4. Which would be the output of the following code snippet:

```
#include<stdio.h>
 int main()
 {
  int main = 110;
  printf(«%d», main);
  return 0;
 }
```

   (a) Generates a syntax error (b) Generates a compile time error
   (c) 110 (d) None of the above
5. C is a general-purpose and ___________ programming language.
   (a) high-level (b) low-level
   (c) assembly (d) machine
6. Which of the following error comes under the syntax error?
   (a) int result= 10/ 'x'; (b) int result= 10/2.3;
   (c) int result= 10+20; (d) int result= 10 20;

ANSWERS											
1.	(d)	2.	(b)	3.	(c)	4.	(a)	5.	(a)	6.	(a)

Short and Long Answer Type Questions

1. Match the following table.

Data Type		Format Specifier	
A	char	1	%lf
B	float	2	%Lf
C	double	3	%c
D	long int	4	%hd
E	unsigned int	5	%f
F	int	6	%lu
G	short int	7	%u
H	signed char	8	%c
I	long double	9	%li
J	unsigned long int	10	%d

2. Find the invalid variable and explain the errors.

NEWCODE	_NEW	new-salary	#MEDIAN
circle.822	fog in 2022	time over	FLOAT
wORld	qu#e$ue.	your'sloss	area # 4
2022_YMonth	1old	+Press	new_*

3. What is a header file? Explain the use of header files in C programs.
4. Can a C program be compiled without a main()? If No, explain why.
5. What is printf() & scanf() in C Program? Explain with an example.
6. Explain the difference between the Interpreter & Compiler. Also, draw the basic process of compilation of a C program.
7. Read statements a) and b) whether they are true or false. Explain your justification.
   - Machine languages are not typically machine-dependent.
   - C is typically assumed to be machine-independent.
8. Print "Welcome to the Learning World" in the following ways:
   - Welcome to the Learning World
   - Welcome

     to

     the

     Learning

     World

9. Write a correct statement for each of the following; if there is no error, write "NO Change".
   - int main{}
   - print("Hello Learner");
   - int variable
   - int x=10 y=20;
   - print("Hello!")
   - #include(stdio.h)
   - char chr = "x";
   - Printf("character = %c" chr);
   - scan("%d", &xyz");
   - #include(stdio)
10. Write an output for the following printf statements; if there is no output, write "None". Assume a = 3 and b = 4.
    - ("%d", a);
    - ("%d", a + a + a);
    - ("a=");
    - ("b=%d", a*a);
    - ("%d = %d", a + b, b + a);
    - /*("a + b + a = %d", b + a + b); */
    - ("\n\n\n\n");

PRACTICAL

1. Write a program to accept two integers from the user after compiling the code, calculate the sum of these integers, and print the outcome using printf.
2. Write a program to accept one integer, one character, and one float by a user at the keyboard, print these values, using printf.
3. Write a program that prints "Computer Programming: Theory and Practicals" in two lines such that "Computer Programming:" in first line and Theory and Practicals in the second line.

KNOW MORE

How to run a C program using GNU Compiler Collection (gcc)

As we know, C is a high-level language which means, you need to translate the source code written in a human-understandable format into a machine-understandable format. Therefore, a compiler is needed to compile the program. GNU Compiler Collection (gcc) is one of the most popular compilers available for compiling C programs. It is available for free.

Here are the steps of compiling and running a c program using gcc.

- Write a C program and save it with .c extension. For example, fProgram.c
- Now, compile this program using gcc command on the terminal/command prompt. For example, gcc fProgram.c -o fProgram

- Run the program by command ./fProgram on Linux and Mac machines and fPrograms on windows machines.

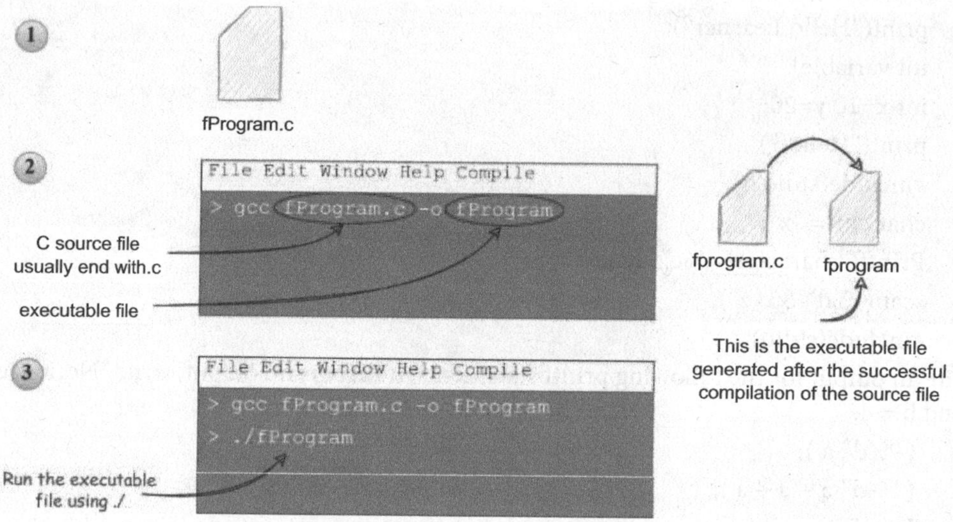

History of Computers

There was a time before computers, even though they are now an integral part of human life. Knowing computers' history and advancement can help us understand the complexity and creativity in computer manufacturing. Computers can be categorized in multiple ways depending on their generation, size, working, and use. There exist four generations of computers. The first-generation computers from 1940-1958 utilized vacuum tubes to design circuitry and magnetic drums for memory. These computers took the entire room to build and were expensive to operate (because of the size and maintenance). Next, the second-generation computers (1959-1964) were based on transistors, developed at AT&T's Bell Labs. A single transistor had replaced around 40 vacuum tubes. They were small, fast, and reliable compared to first-generation computers. During this time, high-level languages like FORTRAN and COBO were developed. The program instructions were stored in memory, transitioning from magnetic drum to magnetic core technology. The initial computers of this generation were designed for the atomic industry. Further, the third generation of computers begins from 1965 to 1970. The third generation of computers was developed using the Integrated Circuits (IC) as its foundation. The same transistor but smaller, mounted on silicon chips were used, which significantly boost the speed and effectiveness of computers. The fourth generation started in 1971. These are microprocessor-based computers. Our immediate environment is filled with fourth-generation computers. This generation used semiconductor memory such as ROM, RAM, etc. Computers of significantly smaller size and more capacity were available in this generation. The fifth generation of computers could be Artificial Intelligence (AI). It makes computers behave like human beings. To read in detail, please refer to QR code.

Read more about computer and history

REFERENCES AND SUGGESTED READINGS

1. Lundqvist, I. Kristina. "Introduction to Computers and Programming." (2004).
2. B. L. Juneja and Anita Seth, Programming for Problem Solving (2019)
3. https://nptel.ac.in/courses/106105171
4. https://nptel.ac.in/courses/106104074
5. https://ocw.mit.edu/courses/6-00-introduction-to-computer-science-and-programming-fall-2008/

2 Operators and Input-Output in C

UNIT SPECIFICS

Through this unit we have discussed the following aspects:

- Use of different operators in C language;
- Classification of operators based on number of operands
- Classification based on role of operator
- To learn precedence and associativity of operators;
- Practice problems on various operators;
- Input and Output in C language;
- Formatted input and output in C language;
- Input and output through files;

All these topics are discussed with detailed examples. Further, if needed, there is reference material attached to each topic. To maintain the curiosity and interest of the readers, this unit also provides video links via QR code for the explanation of each topic. At the end of the unit, various types of exercises are provided that include Multiple Choice Questions (MCQs), output-based questions, practical exercises, etc. Moreover, a list of references and suggested readings are given at the end of the unit.

RATIONALE

In this unit, we extend the introduction to C programming started in the first unit. It begins with the standard input and output in C programming. The syntax and semantics of basic input and output utility functions are discussed. Next, we discuss various types of operators available in C language, which are fundamental elements of solving a computational problem. Next, it gives a brief introduction of input and output through files. Though, this part can be covered later after reading the remaining units. It is added here for the sake of completeness. Through this unit, we answer the two fundamental questions:

1. How to take input and show the output using C programming language?
2. How to write expressions that perform some computations involving different types of operators?

PRE-REQUISITES

Basic Mathematics

UNIT OUTCOMES

List of outcomes of this unit is as follows:

U2-O1: Describe basic C operators

U2-O2: Describe associativity and precedence of various operators

U2-O3: Explain formatted input and output in C programming language

U2-O4: Apply different input and output methods in problem solving

U2-O5: Apply different operators to solve complex problems

Unit-2 Outcomes	EXPECTED MAPPING WITH COURSE OUTCOMES (1- Weak Correlation; 2- Medium correlation; 3- Strong Correlation)					
	CO-1	CO-2	CO-3	CO-4	CO-5	CO-6
U2-O1	3	3	3	-	3	1
U2-O2	1	1	2	2	1	-
U2-O3	2	1	3	1	2	1
U2-O4	-	-	3	1	2	2
U2-O5	3	3	3	-	3	1

2.1 EXPRESSIONS AND OPERATORS IN C

In the first unit, we studied different types of instructions involved in a programming language: Type declaration, Arithmetic instructions, and Control instructions. Various operations may be involved to solve a complex problem. These operations are carried out using various operators. You must have used these operators when studying mathematics, such as +, -, =, and so on. In programming languages, we can use these operators on different operands. Together with the operands, they can be called **expressions.** A simple expression consists of a single constant value, the identifier, or a literal string, or a function. Such kinds of simple or multiple expression enclosed in parentheses is called **primary expression**.

Example: Suppose a programmer wants to develop a program to generate the results of the students of any specific class. For that, he has to calculate total marks obtained, percentages, etc., which will require the arithmetic operator, and storing the results, requires the assignment operator. To find out the grades, programmers will need relational operators. To combine more than one relational operator, he will require logical operators. Thus, we can say that different types of operators are required to solve real-life problems. To solve the different types of problems C programming language supports different types of operators, which we will discuss in this section.

Operators perform specific types of operations between variables, constants, etc. In C language, operators are broadly categorized as:

1. Binary Operators
2. Unary Operators
3. Ternary or Conditional Operators

2.2 BINARY OPERATORS

The operators who perform between two operands or values are known as binary operators. In that, each operator required exactly two variables, values, etc., which are known as **operands**.

Syntax of binary operator

```
First_Operand  Operator  Second_Operand
```

Types of binary operators:

A. Arithmetic operators
B. Assignment operators
C. Relational operators
D. Logical operators
E. Bitwise operators

A. **Arithmetic Operators:** Arithmetic operations are the basic calculation operation like addition, subtraction, multiplication, division, and modulus.
   - **Addition (+):** This operation performs the addition of two numbers.
   - **Subtraction (–):** This operation performs the difference between two numbers.
   - **Multiplication (*):** This operation performs the product of two numbers.
   - **Division (/):** This operation performs the division of its operands. In that, the first left operand is divided by the right operand.
   - **Modulo Operator (%):** It has two operands, left and right. The left operand divides by the right operand. After the division, the remaining number which cannot be further divided will be the result. The modulo operator can be used to find the remainder of the only integer numbers. It means both operands should be in integer form.

> ***Note:*** Various special symbols in C are not used in basic mathematics. The percent (`%`) sign depicts the modulo operator and the asterisk (`*`) depicts the multiplication operator. In C, if we want to multiply two operands `p` and `q`, then it should be written as `p*q`; that is, it requires a multiplication operator (`*`), whereas in algebra, multiplication could have been done by simply writing `pq` but, the C language interprets `pq` as an identifier. Therefore, programming languages explicitly require operators to perform2 operations.

B. **Assignment Operators:** These operators assign value to the variables or the identifiers. When this operator executes, it assigns the right operand's value to the left operand's one. The right operand must be either a constant or a variable, but the left operand must be a variable only (it should never be a constant). After the execution of this operator, the left operand's value is overwritten by the right operand's value which could be either a constant value or a value of another variable. The assignment operators are shown in Table 2.1.

> ***Note:*** The operand addressable (which has a memory address) is known as an lvalue. For example, variables. The operand that cannot be addressable or requires a memory location to store is known as an rvalue. The lvalue can also be used as an rvalue but not vice versa. The assignment operator always expects lvalue as a left operand.

For example:

```
var1=5;     // It is the right expression
```

while

```
5=var1;     // It is wrong because 5 has no identifiable memory address,
               so it can't be an lvalue and it generates an error
               "lvalue required".
```

Table 2.1: Assignment operators in C language

Symbol	Meaning	Examples
=	Assignment	var = 19; It means value assigned to the var.
+=	Summation and assignment	var += var1; It means var = var + var1
-=	Difference and assignment	var -= var1; It means var = var - var1
*=	Product and assignment	var *= var1; It means var = var * var1
/=	Division and assignment	var /= var1; It means var = var / var1
%=	Reminder and assignment	var %= var1; It means var = var % var1

Note: In the C language, the operator '=' is used to assign the value, and '==' is used to compare two values, while in basic mathematics, '=' is used for both purposes (assignment and compare).

Fig. 2.1 shows the demonstration of arithmetic and assignment operators. Here in, line 7 read two integer numbers from the user. Line 8, 10, 12, 14, and 16 perform the addition, subtraction, multiplication, division, and modulo operation, respectively; the assignment operator stores the results in the `add_res`, `sub_res`, `mul_res`, `div_res`, and `mod_res` variables, respectively. Line 9, 11, 13, 15, and 17 display the performed operation's results.

```
1.  #include<stdio.h>
2.  int main()
3.  {
4.      int var1, var2;     //variables to be read from the user
5.      int add_res, sub_res, mul_res, div_res, mod_res;
        // variables used to store the results
6.     printf("Enter two numbers to perform arithmetic operations: ");
7.      scanf("%d %d",&var1, &var2);        //read two integer numbers
8.      add_res = var1 + var2; // Addition operation
9.      printf("The addition of %d and %d is: %d \n",var1,var2,
                add_res);
10. sub_res = var1 - var2;     // Subtraction operation
11. printf("The subtraction of %d and %d is: %d \n",var1,var2,
                sub_res);
12. mul_res = var1 * var2;     // Multiplication operation
13. printf("The multiplication of %d and %d is: %d \n",var1,var2,
               mul_res);
14. div_res = var1 / var2;     // Division operation
15. printf("%d divided %d is: %d \n",var1,var2,div_res);
16. mod_res = var1 % var2;     // Modulo operation
```

```
printf("The mod of %d and %d is: %d \n",var1,var2,mod_res);
return 0;
}
```

Fig 2.1: Demonstration of arithmetic and assignment operators

Output:

```
Enter two numbers to perform arithmetic operations: 74  9
The addition of 74 and 9 is: 83
The subtraction of 74 and 9 is: 65
The multiplication of 74 and 9 is: 666
74 divided 9 is: 8
The mod of 74 and 9 is: 2
```

****Note:*** It is assumed that the user enters 74 and 9 as input.

Note: The arithmetic (except modulo) operator behavior depends on the types of the operand. If both operands are integers, then the results will be an integer. If one of the operands is float type (real number), then the output will be a float type.

Example:

`var=33/2;` //Here divisor and dividend both are integers so the output will be 16 instead of 16.5.

`var=33.0/2;` // Here dividend is the float type (one of the operands is a float type, then the output will be a float type), so here output will be 16.5.

C. **Relational Operator:** These operators show the relation among the two operands. They are also used for decision-making tasks. The relational operators check the condition; if it is true, it returns 1, otherwise returns 0. Table 2.2 contains the different types of relational operators. The demonstration of the relational operators is shown in Fig 2.2.

Table 2.2: Different types of relational operators

Operator	Meaning
Less-than (<) and Greater-than (>) operators:	The operator '>' checks if the left operand's value is greater than right operand's one and returns 1, otherwise returns 0.
Less-than or equal to (<=) and Greater-than or equal to (>=)	Similarly, '<' checks if the left operand's value is smaller than right operand's one and returns 1, otherwise returns 0.
Equal to (==) and Not equal to (!=) operator:	The operator '==' returns 1 when both operands (left and right) are the same (equal to). If not, then it returns 0. The operator '!=' returns 1 when both operands (left and right) are different (not equal to). If not, then it returns 0.

```
#include<stdio.h>
int main()
{
  int var1, var2;
  var1=23;
  var2=32;
  printf(“Enter two numbers to check which relationship exists
          between them:”);
  scanf(“%d%d”, &var1,&var2);
  printf(“%d is Greater-than %d: the result is %d\n”, var1, var2,
         var1>var2);          // Greater-than operator
  printf(“%d is Less-than %d: the result is %d\n”,var1, var2,
          var1<var2);         // Less-than operator
  printf(“%d is Greater than or equal to %d: the result is %d\n”,
       var1,var2,var1>=var2); //Greater-than or equal to operator
  printf(“%d is Less than or equal to %d: the result is %d\n”,
       var1, var2, var2<=var1); // Less than or equal to operator
 printf(“%d equals to %d: the result is %d\n”, var1, var2,
 var1==var2);                // Equal to operator
  printf(“%d is not equal to %d: the result is %d\n”, var1, var2,
          var2!=var1);       // Not equal to operator
  return 0;
}
```

Fig. 2.2: Demonstration of relational operators

Output:

```
Enter two numbers to check which relationship exists between them:23
45
23 is Greater-than 45: the result is 0
23 is Less-than 45: the result is 1
23 is Greater than or equal to 45: the result is 0
23 is Less than or equal to 45: the result is 0
23 equals to 45: the result is 0
23 is not equal to 45: the result is 1
```

****Note:*** It is assumed that the user enters 23 and 45 as an input

D. Logical Operator: Generally, logical operators are used with relational operators. Logical operators are used for combining two statements. Logical operators also return the results as true (`1`) or false (`0`).

Basic different logical operators are:

AND operator (&&): AND operator is used to combine two statements (operands). If both statements are true, then AND operator returns true else, it returns false. Fig. 2.3 shows the demonstration of the logical AND operator.

```
#include<stdio.h>
int main()
{
   int var1, var2;
   var1= 20<30 && 40<50;
   var2= 20<30 && 40>50;
   printf("Result of the first expression is %d\n",var1);
   printf("Result of the second expression is %d\n",var2);
   return 0;
}
```

Fig. 2.3: Demonstration of the logical AND operator

Output:

```
Result of the first expression is 1
Result of the second expression is 0
```

Note: In the AND operator, evaluation of the statements starts from left to right. If the first statement is false, then the AND operator returns false without executing the second statement. The second statement will execute when the first statement is true. As shown in Fig. 2.4.

```
1. #include<stdio.h>
1. int main()
2. {
3.    int var1, var2;
4.    var1=10;
5.    var2= 20>30 && ++var1;
   // ++var1 means var1=var1+1
6.    printf("Results of the expression is %d\n",var2);
7.    printf("Updated value of var1 is %d\n",var1);
8.    return 0;
9. }
```

Fig. 2.4: Demonstration of the logical AND operator

In the above code, in line 5 first statement, 20>30, is false, so AND operator returns false without executing the second statement. Because of this, the value of var1 will remain the same (10). The output is given below.

Output:

```
Results of the expression is 0
Updated value of var1 is 10
```

OR operator (||): The OR operator is used to combine two statements (operands). If any one of the statements is true, then the OR operator returns true else, it returns false. Fig. 2.5 shows the demonstration of the logical OR operator.

```
#include<stdio.h>
int main()
{
   int var1, var2;
   var1= 20>30 || 40>50;
   var2= 20<30 || 40>50;
   printf("value of var1 is %d\n",var1);
   printf("value of var2 is %d\n",var2);
   return 0;
}
```

Fig. 2.5: Demonstration of the logical OR operator

Output:

```
value of var1 is 0
value of var2 is 1
```

Note: In the OR operator, evaluation of the statements starts from left to right. If the first statement is true, then the OR operator returns true without executing the second statement. The second statement will execute when the first statement is false. As shown in Fig. 2.6.

```
#include<stdio.h>
int main()
{
   int var1, var2;
   var1=10;
   var2= 20<30 || ++var1;
 // ++var1 means var1=var1+1
   printf("Results of the expression is %d\n",var2);
   printf("Updated value of var1 is %d\n",var1);
   return 0;
}
```

Fig. 2.6: Demonstration of the logical OR operator

In the above code, at line number 6 first statement, `20<30`, is true, so the `OR` operator returns true without executing the second statement. Because of this, the value of var1 will remain the same (`10`).

Output:

```
Results of the expression is 1
Updated value of var1 is 10
```

NOT operator (!): Logical NOT (!) is an unary operator. It applied to a single statement. The logical not operator complements the results of the statement. It means if the statement is true, then after the not operator, it returns the false. Fig. 2.7 shows the demonstration of the logical `NOT` operator.

```
#include<stdio.h>
int main()
{
   int var1, var2;
   var1= !(20>30);  // 20>30 is false but due to not operator return true
   var2= !(20<30); // 20<30 is true but due to not operator  return false
   printf("Result of !(20>30) is %d\n",var1);
   printf("Result of !(20<30) is %d\n",var2);
   return 0;
}
```

Fig. 2.7: Demonstration of the logical NOT operator

Output:

```
Result of !(20>30) is 1
Result of !(20<30) is 0
```

E. *Bitwise Operator.* The bitwise operators deal with the bit. It means that given operands are converted into the binary form and then manipulated bits according to the operations.

Basic bitwise operators are shown in Table 2.3. The demonstration of the bitwise operators is shown in Fig. 2.8.

Table 2.3: Basic bitwise operators

Operator	Meaning
Bitwise `OR` operator (`|`)	The operator `OR` (`|`) returns `0` if both the bits are `0`, otherwise, it returns `1`.
Bitwise `AND` operator (`&`)	The operator AND (&) returns 1 if both the bits are 1, otherwise, it returns 0.
Bitwise `XOR` operator (`^`)	The operator `XOR` (`^`) returns `0` if both the bits are the same (either `0` or 1), otherwise, it returns `1`.
Bitwise left shift operator (<<)	The `left shift` (<<) operator left shifts the bits of the left operand; the right operand tells the total number of places to be shifted.

Operator	Meaning
Bitwise right shift operator (>>)	The right shift (>>) operator right shifts the bits of the left operand; the right operand tells the total number of places to be shifted.
Bitwise Complement operator (~)	This is the unary operator; this operator is performed on the single operand. The operator '~' flips each bit of the operand. It means 1 becomes 0 and 0 becomes 1.

For example, suppose var1 and var2 holds the binary number 00111 and 01001 respectively then

```
var1 | var2     0   1   1   1   1
var1 & var2     0   0   1   0   1
var1 ^ var2     0   1   0   1   0
var1<<2         1   1   1   0   0
var1>>2         1   1   0   0   1
~var1           1   1   0   0   0
```

```
#include <stdio.h>
int main()
{
   int var1,var2,var3;
   printf("Enter two numbers to perform bitwise operations ");
   scanf("%d%d",&var1,&var2);
   var3= var1 | var2;       // Bitwise OR operation
   printf("The result of the bitwise OR operation between %d and %d
           is: %d \n",var1,var2,var3);
   var3= var1 & var2;       // Bitwise AND operation
   printf("The result of the bitwise AND operation between %d and
           %d is: %d \n",var1,var2,var3);
   var3= var1 ^ var2;       // Bitwise XOR operation
   printf("The result of the bitwise XOR operation between %d and
           %d is: %d \n",var1,var2,var3);
   var3= var1 << 2;        // Bitwise left shift operation
   printf("The result of 2 left shifts operation on %d is: %d \n",
           var1,var3);
   var3= var1 >> 2;        // Bitwise right shift operation
   printf("The result of 2 right shifts operation on %d is: %d \n",
           var1,var3);
   var3= ~var1;          // Bitwise complement operation
   printf("The bitwise complement of %d number is: %d\n",var1,var3);
   return 0;
}
```

Fig. 2.8: Demonstration of the bitwise operators

In the above code, line 6 receives two integer numbers from the user, which are stored in `var1` and `var2` variables; suppose they are 4 and 5. Line numbers 7, 9, 11, 13, 15, and 17 perform the bitwise `OR, AND, XOR, left shift, right shift,` and `complement,` respectively. Before doing the bitwise operation compiler convert the operand into the binary number (the required number of bits vary compiler to compiler, only for the understanding here we take 8 bits), which means `4` becomes `00000100` and `5` becomes `00000101`. Now each bit performed bitwise operation separately; for example, in bitwise `OR` operation (`00000100 | 00000101`), `0|1` generates `1`, `0|0` generates `0`, `1|1` generates `1`. The final results will be `00000101`, which is the `5`. Similarly, all other operations will be performed. The output of the above code is shown below.

Output:

```
Enter two numbers to perform bitwise operations 4 5
The result of the bitwise OR operation between 4 and 5 is: 5
The result of the bitwise AND operation between 4 and 5 is: 4
The result of the bitwise XOR operation between 4 and 5 is: 1
The result of 2 left shifts operation on 4 is: 16
The result of 2 right shifts operation on 4 is: 1
The bitwise complement of 4 number is: -5
```

***Note:** It is assumed that the user enters 4 and 5 as an input

2.3 UNARY OPERATOR

The unary operator requires only one operand or the arguments. Some basic unary operators are as given below.

- ***Unary minus (–):*** It changes the sign of any operands. It means negative becomes positive or positive becomes negative.

  Example: `var1= 19;`

  `var2= -var1` // it means `var2 = -19`

- ***Unary plus (+):*** It is a unary plus operator. It represents the positive sign of the number.

  Example: `var1= +19;` // it means positive 19 assigned to the `var1`

- ***`sizeof()` operator:*** This operator returns the size of the operand in bytes.

  Example: `sizeof(var1);` // Here sizeof() operator returns how many bytes are allotted to the `var1`.

- ***Addressof operator (&):*** The `&` operator is also known as the ampersand operator. It returns the address of memory allotted to the variable.

  Example: `&var1;` // It returns the memory address of the `var1`.

Fig. 2.9 shows the demonstration of the unary operators.

```
#include <stdio.h>
int main()
{
```

```
    int var1,var2;
    printf("Enter a number to perform unary operations ");
    scanf("%d",&var1);
    var2= -var1;          // Unary minus operation
      printf("The number %d becomes %d after the unary minus operation\n",var1,var2);
    var2= +var1;          // Unary plus operation
        printf("The number %d becomes %d after the unary plus operation\n",var1,var2);
                          // addressof operation
      printf("The address of %d is %d \n",var1,&var1);
      var2= sizeof(var1);  // sizeof operation
  printf("The number of bytes required to store %d is %d\n",var1,var2);
      return 0;
  }
```

Fig 2.9 Demonstration of the unary operators

The above code demonstrates the `-`, `+`, `&`, and `sizeof` unary operations. The output of the above code is shown below.

Output:

```
Enter a number to perform unary operations 12
The number 12 becomes -12 after the unary minus operation
The number 12 becomes 12 after the unary plus operation
The address of 12 is 1070816304
The number of bytes required to store 12 is 4
```

*Note: It is assumed that the user enters 12 as an input

- ***Decrement operator (--)***: This operator decrements the value of the variable by 1. Decrement operator can be pre or post-decrement.
- ***Post-decrement*** operator first uses the value of the variable and then decrements the value of the variable by 1.

  Example: `var1=19;`

  `var2= var1++;` // it means first the value of `var1` assigned to the `var2` then decrement the value of `var1` by `1`. After the following statement, the value of `var1` and `var2` will be 18 and 19, respectively.

- ***Pre-decrement*** operator first decrement the value by 1, then use the value of the variable.

  Example: `var1=19;`

  `var2= ++var1;` // it means first the value of `var1` decrement by the 1 and then assign to the `var2`. After the following statement, the value of `var1` and `var2` will be 18 and 18, respectively.

- ***Increment operator (++)***: This operator is used to increment a value of the variable by `1`. Increment operator can be pre or post-increment.
- ***Post-increment*** operator first uses the value of the variable and then increments the value of the variable by 1.

  Example: `var1=19;`

  `var2= var1++;` // it means first the value of var1 assigned to the `var2` then increment the value of `var1` by `1`. After the following statement, the value of `var1` and `var2` will be 20 and 19, respectively.

  Pre-increment operator first increments the value by 1 before using it.

  Example:

  `var1=19;`

  `var2= ++var1;` // it means first the value of `var1` increment by the `1` and then assign to the `var2`. After the following statement, the value of `var1` and `var2` will be 20 and 20, respectively.

A C program demonstrating the unary increment and decrement operators is shown in Fig. 2.10.

```
#include <stdio.h>
int main()
{
    int var1,var2;
    printf("Enter a number to perform pre-increment operation ");
    scanf("%d",&var1);
    printf("The entered number is: %d\n",var1);
    printf("In post-increment operation, the number is printed,
            then incremented. The number is: %d\n", ++var1);
    printf("The updated number is: %d\n\n",var1);
    printf("Enter a number to perform post-increment operation ");
    scanf("%d",&var1);
    printf("The entered number is: %d\n",var1);
    printf("In post-increment operation, the number is printed,
            then incremented. The number is: %d\n", var1++);
    printf("The updated number is: %d\n\n",var1);
    printf("Enter a number to perform pre-decrement operation ");
    scanf("%d",&var1);
    printf("The entered number is: %d\n",var1);
    printf("In a pre-decrement operation, the number is decremented
            and then printed. The number is: %d\n", --var1);
    printf("The updated number is: %d\n\n",var1);
    printf("Enter a number to perform post-decrement operation ");
```

```
21.    scanf("%d",&var1);
22.    printf("The entered number is: %d\n",var1);
23.    printf("In post-decrement operation, the number is printed
              then decrement. The number is: %d\n", var1--);
24.    printf("The updated number is: %d\n",var1);

25.    return 0;
26. }
```

Fig. 2.10: Demonstration of the increment and decrement unary operators

In the above example, line 8 performs a pre-increment operation which first increases the variable's value by 1 and then using the `printf` function displays the value. Line 13 performs a post-increment operation, which first displays the value of the variable by using the `printf` function and then increments it by `1`.

The same procedure is followed in performing the decrement operations; however, the decrement operation decrements the value of the variable by 1. The final output is shown below.

Output:

```
Enter a number to perform pre-increment operation 5
The entered number is: 5
In post-increment operation, the number is printed, then incremented.
The number is: 6
The updated number is: 6
Enter a number to perform post-increment operation 5
The entered number is: 5
In post-increment operation, the number is printed, then incremented.
The number is: 5
The updated number is: 6
Enter a number to perform pre-decrement operation 5
The entered number is: 5
In a pre-decrement operation, the number is decremented and then
printed. The number is: 4
The updated number is: 4
Enter a number to perform post-decrement operation 5
The entered number is: 5
In post-decrement operation, the number is printed then decrement.
The number is: 5
The updated number is: 4
```

***Note:** It is assumed that the user enters 5 as an input

2.4 TERNARY OPERATOR

The operator which requires three operands is known as the ternary operator. The conditional operator is the example of the ternary operator.

Conditional operator (?:): The conditional operator is the operator which requires three operands. The symbol of the conditional operator is '? :'. The conditional operator divides into three parts: left, middle, and right using '?' and ':' symbols. The left operand represents the condition, middle and right operands represent the true and the false parts. If the expression in the conditional part returns true, then the middle part will execute, and the right part will skip. If the expression returns false, then the right operand will execute, and the middle part will skip. The demonstration of the ternary operator is shown in Fig. 2.11.

Syntax of the conditional operator:

```
conditional_operand ? middle_operand : right_operand
```

Example: `var1= 23>12 ? 23 :12;` //The value of `var1` will be 23.
`var2= 23<12 ? 23 :12` // The value of `var2` will be 12.

```
#include <stdio.h>
int main()
{
 int var1, var2, var3;
  var1= 23<19?23:19; // conditional part is false, so the expression
                        returns the right operand (19)
   var2= 45>29?45:29; // conditional part is true, so the expression
                         returns the left operand (45)
    printf("var1= %d\n",var1);
    printf("var2= %d\n",var2);
   return 0;
}
```

Fig. 2.11: Demonstration of the ternary operator

Output:

```
var1= 19
var2= 45
```

2.5 IMPLICIT AND EXPLICIT-TYPE CONVERSIONS

Converting one data type into another is known as type conversion. Type conversion can be done in two ways:

1. Implicit type conversion
2. Explicit type conversion

2.5.1 Implicit Type Conversion

This is done automatically by the compiler. When the compiler receives two different types of operands then it converts the lower data type into the higher data type. Fig. 2.12 shows the list of data types from lower to higher with respect to memory size. The demonstration of the implicit type conversion is shown in Fig. 2.13.

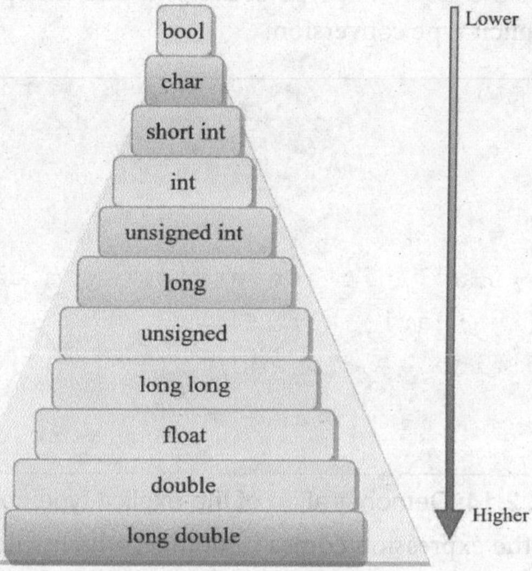

Fig. 2.12: Data types from top to bottom in increasing order of memory size.

```
1. #include<stdio.h>
2. int main()
3. {
4.     int var1 = 19;      // integer var1
5.     char var2 = ‘A’;   // character var2
6.    // var2 implicitly converted to int. ASCII value of ‘A’ is 65
7.     var1 = var1 + var2;
8.     // var1 is implicitly converted to float
9.     float var3 = var1 + 1.0;
10.      printf(“var1 = %d, var3 = %f”, var1, var3);
11.      return 0;
12.   }
```

Fig. 2.13: Demonstration of the implicit type conversion

In the above example, the implicit type conversion has done in lines 7 and 9. Following is the output of the code:

Output:

```
var1 = 84, var3 = 85.000000
```

2.5.2 Explicit Type Conversion

In this process, the data type is changed by the user. In this user can typecast the result into the particular data type. This process is also known as type casting. The syntax is as given below.

```
(type) expression
```

Here expression returns the result and type converts it into the specific data type. Fig. 2.14 shows the demonstration of the explicit type conversion.

```
1. #include<stdio.h>
2. int main()
3. {
4.       double var1 = 1.7;
                   // Explicit conversion from double to int
5.       int add = (int)var1 + 3;
6.       printf("addition = %d", add);
7.       return 0;
8. }
```

Fig. 2.14: Demonstration of the explicit type conversion

In line 5, the result of the expression comes in double, which will explicitly convert into the `int`. The output of the above code is:

Output:

```
addition = 4
```

Operators in C have a unique meaning to make the programming language unambiguous. Moreover, there are some rules and syntax to use these operators. Now, we will discuss the precedence and associativity of these operators.

2.6 PRECEDENCE AND ASSOCIATIVITY OF C OPERATORS

When an expression contains multiple operators, the execution of operators is decided based on their precedence. The precedence of operators tells whether the given operators are executed first or later. The associativity of the operator shows the direction (left to right or right to left) of the execution of the operation. Associativity will check when two or more operators with the same precedence participate in the same expression. Fig. 2.15 shows the precedence and the associativity of the C operators.

Question 2.1: How hierarchy of operators work?

The execution of the expression (which contains several operations) depends on the priority and associativity of the operators. This section includes examples to understand the hierarchy of the operators.

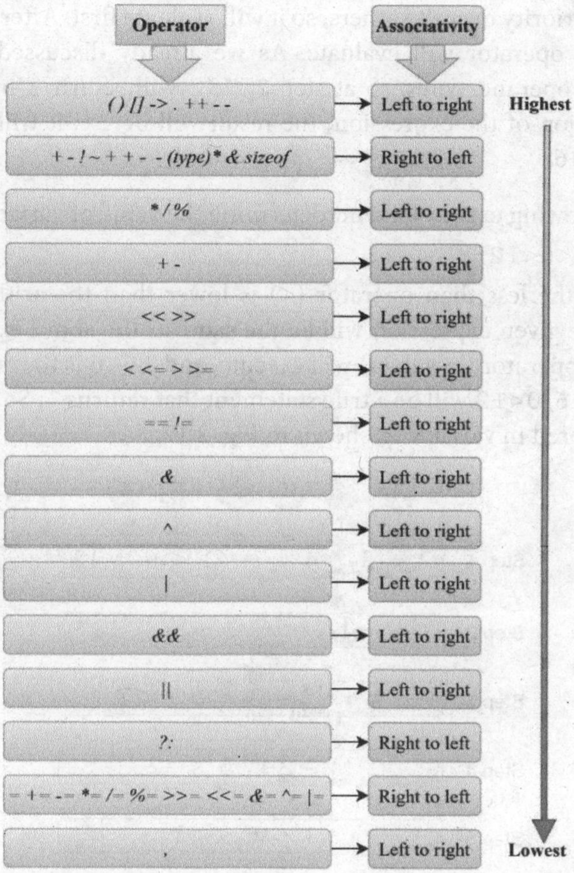

Fig. 2.15: Precedence and the associativity of the operators

Example: Evaluate the following expression and determine the value of variable x.

`x=2+3*4-7/2;`

Solution: Before executing the expression, the compiler finds the operator's execution sequence based on the operators' priority and associativity; in this example, the multiplication operator (*)

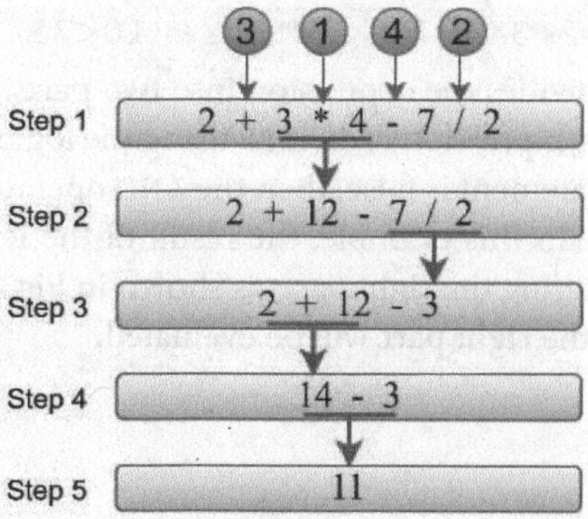

Fig. 2.16: Evaluation of `x=2+3*4-7/2`

has the highest priority over the others, so it will evaluate first. After it, the division, addition, and subtraction operator will evaluate. As we already discussed, the operator behavior depends on the operand types, so at step 2, 7/2 will return 3 instead of 3.5. After the complete execution of the expression, the result will be 11; it will be stored in variable x, shown in Fig. 2.16.

Example: Evaluate the following expression and determine the value of variable x.

```
x=2+3*4-7/2<6<12;
```

Solution: The priority of the less than operator (<) is lower than the arithmetic operators, so the evaluation of the given expression will be the same as the above example till step 5. At step 5, the relational operator (less than) will execute, and 11<6 is the false statement, which will return 0. At step 6, 0<12 will be a true statement that returns 1. So, the final result will be 1, which will be stored in variable x, shown in Fig. 2.17.

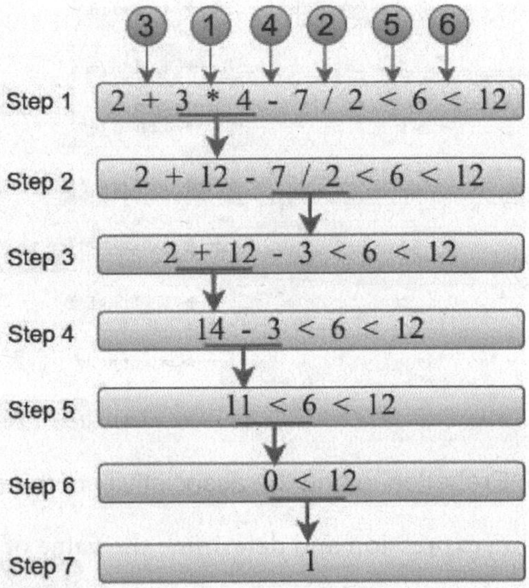

Fig. 2.17: Evaluation of x=2+3*4-7/2<6<12

Example: Evaluate the following expression and determine the value of variable x.

```
x=2+3*4-7/2<6<12 && 10<71/6;
```

Solution: The logical operator divides the expression into two parts: left and right. Evaluation is done from left to right. This expression is divided using the logical AND operator (&&); In the AND operator, If the first statement is false, then the AND operator returns false without executing the second statement. In this example, the result of the left part is 0, so AND operator will return 0 without executing the right part, as shown in Fig. 2.18. If the value of the left part is true (non-zero) then the right part will be evaluated.

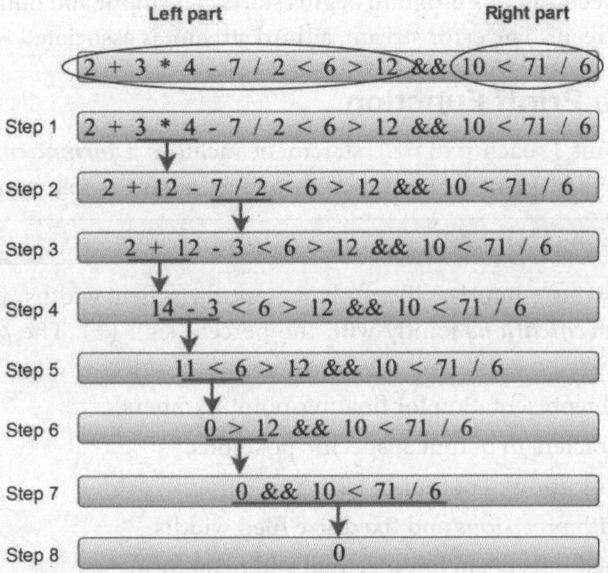

Fig. 2.18: Evaluation of x=2+3*4-7/2<6<12 && 10<71/6

2.7 INPUT AND OUTPUT IN C PROGRAMMING

In the first unit, we had an introduction to problem-solving through computers. We studied the fundamentals of programming languages and introduction to C programming. In any problem-solving approach, input and output are key aspects.

> ***Example:*** Assume one software/application/machine is built to tell you the name of the capital of a country i.e., you give (**input**) the name of the country and the machine will tell (**output**) the capital name. There could be different possible ways available to give input to the machine. For example, you might tell the machine via voice command (through microphone) or by typing input in the machine via the attached keyboard.

Thus, when a programmer writes a program in any programming language, then the programmer must specify how it will take the input and how it will show or give the output. In Unit I, we discussed the various input-output devices. In the C programming language, we have the facility (through built-in functions) to take input via the input device and show the output through the output devices. In computers, the standard keyboard is considered a standard input device, and the monitor (screen) is considered a standard output device.

In unit-I, we introduced two basic utility functions `printf` and `scanf` to take input data from the standard input device (keyboard) and show output data through the standard output device (Monitor). We will discuss the input and output in C programming in detail.

Input and Output Stream. In computers, every input and output operation is carried out using a sequence of bytes called streams. Bytes are transferred from an input device (such as a keyboard, mouse, or scanner) to the main memory during input operations. In contrast, bytes are transferred from the main memory to a device during output operations. Three streams are automatically linked to the program whenever the execution of a program begins starts. The input and output stream has associated with the keyboard and screen. The error stream, a third stream, is associated with the screen.

2.7.1 Output with Printf Function

As we have studied in Unit 1, each `printf` statement includes a ***format control string*** describing a format in which output will be printed. The function `printf` has the following syntax.

```
printf( format_control_string, other parameters);
```

The format control string comprises literal characters, flags, field widths, and conversion specifiers, these form ***conversion specifications*** jointly with the percent sign (`%`). The ***printf*** does the following formatting:

1. Using exponential representation for floating-point numbers.
2. Placing literal characters in output at specific positions.
3. Left and right justification of outputs.
4. *Displaying data with precisions and fixed size filed widths.*
5. Displaying unsigned integers in hexadecimal and octal formats.
6. Rounding off a floating point numbers into a fixed number of decimal places.
7. Arranging a column of values, so the decimal points are stacked on top of the other.

format_control_string describes a format in which output will be printed, and the *additional_parameters* are optional parameters corresponding to conversion specification in *format_control_string.* The conversion specification consist of a percent sign at the starting followed by a conversion specifier at the end. One format control string can contain many conversion specifications.

2.7.1.1 Printing Integers and Floating-point Numbers

An ***integer*** is a number that is written without a fractional part—for example, `-54, 9,` or `254`. There are many formats to display an integer value shown in Table 2.4. Similarly, a **floating-point** number contains a fractional part (decimal point). For eg., `45.12, -567.334`, or `0.0`. The floating-point number is represented in fixed point notation using the specifier `f` whereas in the exponential form notation using the specifier `e` (or `E`) ('exponent'). The lowercase `e` prints *lowercase* `e` and `E` prints *uppercase* `E`. It is equivalent to mathematics scientific notation. For instance, the number `1320.23` is depicted as

$$1.32023 \times 10^3$$

in scientific notation, whereas

```
1.32023E+03
```

in exponent notation by the computer system. The values printed using the specifiers `e, f,` and `E` displays by default six precision digits followed by a decimal point. The floating-point number is represented either in exponential or fixed-point notation depending upon the value of magnitude with no trailing zeros. For example,

```
1.2023000 is printed as 1.2023 // with no trailing zero.
```

The values are displayed with `E` or (`e`) if their exponent is less than `-4` after being converted to exponential notation or if their exponent is greater than or equal to the six precision digits and in rest of the cases, the value is printed using the conversion specifier `f`. The decimal point is always at least one digit to the left of all the floating point specifiers. The numbers `0.00000456`, `456`, `4.56`, `45.60`, and `4560000.0` are displayed as `4.56e-06`, `456`, `4.56`, `45.6`, and `4.56+e06` using the specifier 'g'.

```
The number 0.00000456 is written in exponential notation since the exponent (-6) is smaller than -4, and the number 4560000.0 also uses exponential notation since the exponent (6) is equal to the default precision (six precision digits).
```

A lowercase `g` results in the output of a lowercase `e`, whereas an uppercase `G` results in the output of an uppercase `E` (same as the distinction between `e` and `E`). The number is rounded in the output while using the conversion specifiers `%e`, `%E`, and `%g`, but not when using the conversion specifier `%f`.

Table 2.4: Integer and Floating-point Conversion Specifiers

Conversion Specifier	Description
Integer Numbers	
`d`	Representing a signed integer.
`i`	Representing a signed integer (The specifier `d` and `i` have different interpretations when used with `scanf` function)
`u`	Representing an unsigned integer.
`o`	Representing an unsigned octal integer.
`X or x`	Representing an unsigned hexadecimal integer.
`l or h`	`l` and `h` are length modifiers and indicate that long and short integers are shown when placed before any integer conversion specifier.
Floating-point Numbers	
`f`	Representing fixed-point notation.
`E or e`	Representing exponential notation.
`G or g`	Representing a number either in fixed or exponential notation, depending upon the magnitude of the value.

```
#include <stdio.h>
int main( )
{                     /* Integer conversion specifiers */
  printf("%d \n", 254 );
  printf("%d \n", -254 );  // prints a number along with the minus sign
```

```
printf("%d \n", +254 ); // hides the plus sign and.prints a number only
printf("%i \n", 254 );
printf("%o \n", 254 );
printf("%u \n", 254 );
printf("%u \n", -254 );   //-254 is converted to the unsigned value 4294967042
printf("%X \n", 254 );
printf("%x \n", 254 );
printf("%hd \n", 2500 );
printf("%ld \n", 2000000000 );
            /* Floating-point  conversion specifiers */
printf("%f \n", 9876543.21 );
printf("%e \n", 9876543.21 );
printf("%E \n", 9876543.219 );
printf("%E \n", -9876543.219 );
printf("%g \n", 9876543.21 );
printf("%G \n", 9876543.21 );

return 0;
}
```

Fig. 2.19: Demonstration the use of various integer and floating-point conversion specifiers

Output:

```
254
-254
254
254
376
254
4294967042
FE
fe
2500
250000000
9876543.210000
9.876543e+06
9.876543E+06
```

```
-9.876543E+06
9.87654e+06
9.87654E+06
```

2.7.1.2 Printing Strings and Characters

There are two conversion specifiers, `c` and `s`, for printing characters and strings. A char argument '`%c`' is required for conversion specifier `c` whereas, '`%s`' is required for conversion specifier `s`. According to the specifier `s`, characters are displayed till a null character is encountered (`'\0'`). The following program (Fig. 2.20) displays a character and string using specifiers:

```
#include <stdio.h>
int main()
{
    char  A =  'C' ;
    char  B[] = "C program";
    printf("%c\n", A);
    printf("%s\n", "C Program");
    printf("%s\n", B);
    return 0;
}
```

Fig. 2.20: Demonstration the use of string and character conversion specifier

Output:

```
C
C Program
C program
```

2.7.2 Escape Sequence

We can see from the above program that the character `\n` was not printed on the screen despite being written in the `printf` statement. The backslash (\) used in the printf statement is called the escape character. So, an escape sequence is a sequence of characters that starts with a backslash followed by some character. It is used for formatting the output displayed on the screen. For example, `\n` depicts a new line. This new line character is used to move the cursor to the starting of the following line. Some of the commonly used escape sequences are as shown in Table 2.5:

Table 2.5: Commonly used escape sequences

Escape Sequence	Description
`\n` (New line)	It moves the cursor to the start of the next line.
`\t` (Horizontal tab)	It moves the cursor to one tab horizontal space.

Escape Sequence	Description
\a (Alert)	It generates a sound to alert the programmer about the execution of a program.
\\ (Backslash)	It displays the backslash character in the output.
\" (Double Quote)	It displays a double quote character in the output.

There are other escape sequences available in the C programming language. For further reading you can scan the QR code.

2.7.3 Field widths and Precision in `printf`

Field width describes the size of the field where the data is displayed. The data displayed will be right justified if the field width is greater than the data that will be printed. All conversion specifiers allow the usage of field widths. The program below (Fig. 2.21) is used to show the field widths.

```
#include <stdio.h>
int main( )
{
    printf("%3d\n", 5 );
    printf("%3d\n", 56);
    printf("%3d\n", 567 );
    printf("%3d\n", 5678 );
    printf("%3d\n", -5 );   //minus sign takes one character
                              position in the field width
    printf("%3d\n", -56 );
    printf("%3d\n", -567 );
    printf("%3d\n", -5678 );
    return 0;
}
```

Fig. 2.21: Demonstration the concept of field width

Output:

```
Output:
  5
 56
567
5678
 -5
-56
-567
-5678
```

Precision. In addition, the `printf` function controls the output's precision. For various forms of data, precision has varying implications. The precision defines the minimum number of digits to be shown while using the integer conversion specifier. The zeros are added to the value to be printed until a total number of digits becomes equal to the precision. The value of precision is written between the conversion specifier and percent sign. We can combine both precision and field width in a single `printf` statement by keeping the field width followed by the precision value. A decimal point is used to separate the field width and precision value. The example is shown below:

```
printf("%8.2f", 321.54768);
```

which displays output `321.54` in eight-digit field having two digits in the right of the decimal point.

2.8 INPUT USING SCANF FUNCTION

As we have already studied the basic syntax of `scanf` in unit 1. The `scanf` command has a format control string that comprises literal characters and conversion specifiers and defines the input data's format. The input formatting possibilities of `scanf` function include

1. Entering data of different types.
2. Entering particular characters from a stream of input.
3. Omitting particular characters from a stream of input.

Syntax of *scanf* Function

```
scanf(format_control_string, other parameters);
```

The program (Fig. 2.22) accepts integers as an input using different integer conversion specifiers and shows corresponding decimal integers as an output.

```
#include <stdio.h>
int main()
{
    int x1;
    int x2;
    int x3;
    int x4;
    int x5;
    int x6;
    int x7;
    printf("Enter the value of variables from x1 to x7 : " );
    scanf("%d%o%x%u%i%i%i",&x1, &x2, &x3, &x4, &x5, &x6, &x7
    );
    printf("Entered value of variables displayed as decimal
          integers are:\n");
```

```
    printf("%d%d%d%d%d%d%d\n", x1, x2, x3, x4, x5, x6, x7);
    return 0;
}
```

Fig. 2.22: Demonstration of the integer conversion specifiers

Output:

```
Enter the value of variables from x1 to x7 : -20
20
30
40
50
060
0x80
Entered value of variables displayed as decimal integers are:
-20 16 48 40 50 48 128
```

**Note:* It is assumed that the user enters `-20, 20, 30, 40, 50, 060,` and `0x80` as an input

Integers in decimal, octal, and hexadecimal forms can be entered using conversion specifier %i. Similarly, floating point numbers can be entered using `e`, `E`, `f`, `g`, and `G` conversion specifiers, whereas strings and characters are entered using `s` and `c` conversion specifiers.

2.9 INPUT AND OUTPUT FROM FILES

Apart from taking input from a standard input device and output from a standard output device, the input and the output can be given through files. The data stored in variables are temporary, as the data becomes lost on the program's termination. The files are used for keeping the data permanently. Computer system stores files on secondary memory like a hard disk. In the next section, we'll discuss how a file is created and processed by a C program.

2.9.1 What is a File?

A file is a source where software saves information/data as a series of bytes on a hard disk (secondary storage device). The data stored in the file is permanent. A user can execute different operations on a file, like creating, opening, reading, and updating the data inside the file. The basic functions of handling a file in C are shown in Table 2.6:

Table 2.6: The basic functions of handling a file in C

Function Name	Detail
fopen()	It is used to open an existing file or create a new file.
fclose()	It is used to close a file
fprint()	It is used to write data in a file
fscanf()	It is used to read data from a file

Note: It is essential to understand that while interacting with different files in a program, we must define a file-type pointer. For more details about pointers please go through the QR Code.

2.9.2 File Operations

1. **Create or open an existing file.** A `fopen()` function is used to open an existing file or new file. This function is available in the header file `stdio.h`. The syntax of the `fopen()` function is as follows:

```
file_ptr = fopen(" filename", " mode");
```

`fopen()` takes two parameters filename and mode where filename is the name of the file which needs to be opened and mode defines the mode of access of a file. This function returns the file pointer.

```
fileptr = fopen("/Users/CSE/Desktop/program_file.txt", "w")
// creating a  file "program_file.txt"
```

- Here, if the file `program_file.txt` does not exist in the location `/Users/CSE/Desktop`, then the function creates a file named `program_file.txt` and opens it for writing purposes (mode of access of a file is "*w*"). Various modes are available for file operations such as, *w, r, a, r+, a+, and w+*.
- The "*w*" mode enables a programmer to edit or create the content of a file.
- The "*r*" mode enables a programmer to read the content of a file.
- The "*a*" mode enables a programmer to open a file in append mode.

2. **Close a file.** A *fclose()* function closes a file that was opened for some operations. To close a file, the following syntax is used.

```
fclose(" file_ptr");
```

where `file_ptr` is the file pointer linked to the file that needs to be closed.

```
fclose(fileptr);
```

3. **To read and write the data to the file:** The functions `fscanf()` and `fprintf()` are used for reading and writing the data to the file. These functions are primarily the file versions of `scanf()` and `printf()`, and both require a pointer pointing to the file. The program shows how to write a number to a file (shown in Fig. 2.23).

```
#include<stdio.h>
#include<stdlib.h>
int main()
{
```

```
    int number;
    File *fileptr;
        /* Writing a number to a file */
    fileptr = fopen("/Users/CSE/Desktop/program_file.txt", "w");
                                //opening a file with write mode
    printf("Enter the number to added in a file");
    scanf("%d", &number);
    fprintf(fileptr, "%d", number); // writing a number to the
    file
    fclose(fileptr); //closing the file 'program_file.txt'
    pointing by fileptr
return 0;
        }
```

Fig. 2.23: Demonstration of the writing a file

The above program writes the number inputted by the user and stores it in the file `program_file.txt`. Once we execute this program, the file will contain the inputted number. Now, the next program shows how to read a number from the file and use it in the program (Fig. 2.24).

```
#include<stdio.h>
#include<stdlib.h>
int main()
{
    int number;
    File *fileptr;
        /* Reading a number from a file */
    fileptr = fopen("/Users/CSE/Desktop/program_file.txt", "r");
                        //opening a file with read mode
    fscanf(fileptr, " %d", &number); // reading a number from
                                        the file
    printf("The number is %d" , number);
    fclose(fileptr); //closing the file 'program_file.txt'
  pointing by fileptr
    return 0;
}
```

Fig. 2.24: Demonstration of reading a file

This program reads a number from the program_file.txt and prints the same number on the monitor screen as the output.

UNIT SUMMARY

Operators in C

- In C, if we want to multiply two operands `p` and `q`, then it should be written as `p*q`; that is, it requires a multiplication operator (`*`), whereas in algebra, multiplication could have been done by simply writing `pq` but, the C language interprets `pq` as an identifier. Therefore, programming languages explicitly require operators to perform.
- The operators used in arithmetic operations are binary.
- The two integer operand results in an integer result in the case of a division operation. For example, `11/5` results `2`.
- C supports a modulo operator %, which evaluates the remainder after the division of two integer numbers. For instance, `12%5` results in `2` as a remainder when `12` is divided by `5`. Similarly, `28%7` results in `0` as the remainder.
- In C, when a number is divided by zero it causes immediate termination of a program and generates a compile-time error. Compile time errors do not allow the program to execute whereas run-time errors allow programs to execute but result in incorrect results.
- For ease of programming, C uses a single-line format to write arithmetic expressions. For instance, "a multiplied by b" should be interpreted as `a*b` so that both operator and operands lie in a straight single line.
- The use of parentheses is the same in both C and algebraic expressions. It basically groups the terms together.
- The C language follows the operator precedence rule to compute the arithmetic expressions as followed by algebra.
- The precedence of division, multiplication, and remainder operation is higher than addition and subtraction operators. If there are multiple operators present in an expression, then a precedence rule is applied to evaluate them.
- When an expression consists of more than one operator having same precedence, then they are evaluated from left-to-right - **Associativity**. Some of the operators follow right-to-left associativity also.
- The precedence of all the relational operators is the same and follows left-to-right associativity. Similarly, the assignment operator's associativity is from left to right and has lower precedence than relational operators.
- The equality (==) and assignment (=) operators are different. The equality operator belongs to the relational operator category and is used to check the equality of first and second operands. Whereas the assignment operator belongs to the arithmetic operator category and assigns the right-hand operand value to the left-hand operand.

Input Output in C

- Every input and output operation is carried out using a sequence of bytes called streams.
- `printf` statement includes a format control string describing a format in which output will be printed. It consists of literal characters, flags, field widths, and conversion specifiers.

- Integers are represented using various conversion specifiers such as `d`, `i`, `u`, `o`, and `x`.
- For integers (signed and unsigned), octal integers, and hexadecimal integers. The long and short integers are represented using the modifier `l` or `h`, which are prefixed with the conversion specifier.
- Floating-point numbers are represented using various conversion specifiers such as `e` and `f` for exponential and floating-point notation. The conversion specifier `g` prints either in exponential or fixed-point notation, depending upon the value of an exponent. If the value is greater than or equal to precision and is less than `-4` or then we choose exponential notation.
- Characters and strings are printed using `c` and `s` specifiers.
- Escape sequences are used for formatting the output displayed on the screen. The backslash (\) used in the `printf` statement is called the escape character.
- Field width represents the actual field size where data has to be printed. The printed data can be right justified if the data to be printed is smaller than the field width.
- The precision specifies the number of digits to be displayed when used with `g` specifier. Whereas it specifies the minimum number of digits to be shown when used with an integer specifier.
- `Scanf` function is used for accomplishing the input formatting.
- Integers can be entered using conversion specifiers such as `d`, `i`, `u`, `o`, and `x` for integers (signed and unsigned), octal integers, and hexadecimal integers. Similarly, floating point numbers can be entered using `e`, `f`, and `g` conversion specifiers, whereas strings and characters are entered using `s` and `c` conversion specifiers.

Input-output through files

- A file is a source where software saves information/data as a series of bytes on a hard disk (secondary storage device). Files are used for keeping the data permanently.
- There are various file operations like creating, opening, reading, updating and closing a file.
- `fopen` function is used to open an existing file or new file. `fclose` function closes a file that was opened for some operations.
- `fscanf` and `fprintf` functions are used for reading and writing the data to the file.

EXERCISES

Multiple Choice Questions

1. For a standard program, the input is accepted by using __________.
   (a) files
   (b) scanf and Command-line
   (c) Both (a) and (b)
   (d) None of the above
2. Select the correct method to obtain the user input (integer) value and store it in a xyz variable.
   (a) scanf(%d, &xyz);
   (b) scanf("%s", &xyz);
   (c) scanf("%d", &xyz);
   (d) scanf(%s, &xyz);

3. Let us assume we have used float variable *money* to store *money* in the Indian rupee that we want to display in classic banknotes format (ex. ₹ 3.75). Which statement of printf() will correctly display that *money?*
   (a) printf("*Money*: ₹%d", *money*);
   (b) printf(*Money*: ₹%f, *money*);
   (c) printf("*Money*: ₹", %f, *money*);
   (d) printf("*Money*: ₹%0.2f", *money*);

4. Which is the correct order of precedence of arithmetic operators (from highest to lowest)?
   (a) +, -, %, *, /
   (b) %, *, /, +, –
   (c) %, +, /, *, –
   (d) %, +, -, *, /

5. Which of the following are the correct C statements corresponding to the equation $p = bq^4 + 9$?
   (a) p = b * q * q * q* q + 9;
   (b) p = b * q* q * q* (q + 9);
   (c) p = (b * q) * q * q * (q + 9);
   (d) p = (b * q) * q* q* q + 9;

ANSWERS									
1.	(c)	2.	(c)	3.	(d)	4.	(b)	5.	(a)

Output-based Questions

1. Write the output of the following programs. (Assume every program contains header file *#include<stdio.h>*)

A

```
int main(){
int int var1 main(){
int int var1 = 8;
printf("Number=%d",var1+
                    (var1==8));
return 0;
```

B

```
int main(){
  int var2;
  printf("Enter an integer: ");
  scanf("%d", &var2);
  printf("Number = 4,%d",var2);
  return 0;
}
```

C

```
int main()
{
          float var1;
     int var22;
     printf("Enter var1: ");
     scanf("%f", &var1);
     printf("Enter var2: ");
     scanf("%d", &var2);
     printf("var1 = %f\n", var1);
     printf("var2 = %d", var2);
     return 0;
}
```

D

```
int main()
{
   int var1 = 5, var2;
    var2 = var1;
    printf(«var2 = %d, «, var2);
    var2 += var1;
    printf(«var2 = %d, «, var2);
    var2 -= var1;
    printf(«var2 = %d, «, var2);
    var2 *= var1;
    printf(«var2 = %d, «, var2);
    var2 /= var1;
```

```
    printf(«var2 = %d, «, var2);
    var2 %= var1;
    printf(«var2 = %d», var2);
     return 0;
}
```

E

```
int main()
{
    int jkl = 10;
    printf(«%d», klj);
    return 0;
}
```

F

```
int main()
{
    int var1=2,var2=4,var3=6,var4;
    var4 =var3>var2>var1;
    printf("%d",var4);
    return 0;
}
```

G

```
int main(){
        int t = 1, q = -1, r = 0, s;
        s = ++t && ++q || r -;
        printf("%d",s);
        return 0;
}
```

H

```
int main(){
        int p = 10;
        int q =6*2+5*4<p*3?6:4;
        printf("%d ", q);
        return 0;
}
```

Answers of Output-based Questions	
A. 9	B. Number = 4, 5
C. no1 = 2.000000, no2 = 3	D. y = 5, y = 10, y = 5, y = 25, y = 5, y = 0
E. compile-time error	F. 0
G. 0	H. 4

Short and Long Answer Type Questions

1. Write a C statement to complete separately of the following assignments.
   (a) Define two variables *sub* and *y* of type float
   (b) Store value *25 to* variable *y.*
   (c) Store value *10 to* a variable *sub.*
   (d) Subtract variable *y* from the variable *sub* and store the result in the variable *sub.*
   (e) Print the obtained result.
   (f) Print `1000` in octal form preceded by `0`.
   (g) Print 567.3579 with positive (+) and negative (–) sign using exponential notation with 3 digits of precision.
   (h) Print `34567` left justified in an 8-digit field.

2. Match the following and also write the associativity of each operator

Operators		Type	
A.	++ (postfix) -- (postfix)	1.	assignment
B.	+ - (type) ++ (prefix) -- (prefix)	2.	unary
C.	/ * %	3.	postfix
D.	-	4.	equality
E.	> < >= <=	5.	conditional
F.	!= ==	6.	relational
G.	?:	7.	multiplicative
H.	= -= /= += *= %=	8.	additive

3. Fill in the blanks.

(a) The ________ and ________ conversion specifiers are used for printing characters and strings.

(b) The *E*, *f* and *e* conversion specifiers display ________ digits of precision.

(c) The functions used for input and output formatting is ________ and ________.

(d) The ________ and ________ conversion specifiers are used to show signed decimal integers.

(e) The expression *10=b;* causes ________ error.

(f) The output of the arithmetic expression *7*3/(3+2*3/2)+9*(10/5)* is ________.

(g) The output of the logical expression *! (x > 10) && (y == 2)* is ________, where *x=10* and *y=2*.

Answers			
(a) %c, and %s	(b) 6	(c) scanf and printf	(d) %d and %i
(e) Compile time error	(f) 21	(g) 1	

PRACTICAL

1. There is an IT firm that pays assistants on a commission basis. The commission is 25% of the monthly gross sale with an additional amount of ₹ 1200 monthly. Write a C program to compute the commission and prints it. For example, an assistant made a sale of ₹ 65000.00 in a month. The commission obtained is 25% of 65000 + 1200, which is ₹ 17450.00.

Example of input/output is given below.

```
Enter sales in Rupee: 50000.00
Earning is: ₹ 13700.00

Enter sales in Rupee: 45040.00
Earning is: ₹ 12460.00
```

2. Write a program to apply arithmetic operations (such as add, subtract, multiply, etc.) on two numbers taken by the user and print their results.
3. Display the numbers from 5 to 10 in the same line using:
   (i) A single `printf` *statement* along with six specifiers.
   (ii) A `printf` statement without specifiers.
   (iii) Six `printf` statements.
4. Display the following patterns using the C language. (Hint: use `printf` statements with proper escape sequence to print the pattern).

a)	b)

<pre>*
* *
* * *
* * * *
* * * * *</pre>
	<pre> *
	      * *
	    * * *
	  * * * *
	* * * * *</pre>

KNOW MORE

History of Programming languages: The primary building block of the modern IT industry is a programming language. It is the collection of instructions and directives humans offer computers to carry out a specific job. But did you know that the development of programming languages has a long and colorful chronology?

About five hundred languages are used in the computer industry for programming, each with its unique syntax and capabilities. And if you enter who is the father of the computer, the search engine would point you in Charles Babbage's direction, although he did not create the first line of code. Ada Lovelace constructed the first language for programming in the year 1883. Later on, some well-known languages came into the picture.

High-level programming languages also have a long history that starts with describing the first computers and ends with trendy tools for creating software. As early programming languages were very specialized and relied on syntax that was equally arcane and based on mathematical logic. The research conducted during the mid-twentieth century on compiler theory. And, developer introduces High-level programming languages, which convey instructions using a more approachable syntax.

Between 1942 and 1945, Konrad Zuse developed Plankalkül, the first high-level programming language. In 1951, Corrado Böhm developed the first high-level language with a companion compiler (for his doctoral dissertation). FORTRAN, Formula TRANslation, was created in 1956 by a group working in IBM under the direction of John Backus (published in 1956).

The following important languages were created in following years:

Year of release	Name	Year of release	Name
1949	Assembly Language	1991	Python
1952	Autocode	1991	Visual Basic
1957	FORTRAN	1993	R
1958	ALGOL	1995	JAVA
1959	COBOL	1995	PHP
1964	BASIC	1995	JavaScript
1970	Pascal	1995	Ruby
1972	C	2000	C#
1972	SQL	2006	PowerShell
1978	MATLAB	2009	GO
1983	Objective-C, C++	2011	Kotlin
1990	Haskell	2014	Swift

Scan QR code for further information

REFERENCES AND SUGGESTED READINGS

1. Deitel, P. J. (2015). *C how to Program: With an Introduction to C++ (**Chapter 2**)*. Pearson Education India.
2. David Griffiths and Dawn Griffiths (2011). Head First C, O'Reilly Media, Inc
3. https://nptel.ac.in/courses/106104128
4. https://nptel.ac.in/courses/106105171 (*lectures for week 2 and week 3)*

Dynamic QR Code for Further Reading

The author has created supporting video lectures for each unit. Readers are encouraged to watch the lectures to better understand the topics covered in Unit II. However, it is advised to read the book unit first and then see the videos. The video lectures may not cover the whole unit but are added as supplementary material.

3 Control Statements in C

UNIT SPECIFICS

Through this unit we have discussed the following aspects:

- Need of control statements in programming;
- Types of control statements in C;
- Syntax and semantics of different Selection statements;
- Practice problems on selection statements: if, if…else, switch;
- Syntax and semantics of different repetition statements;
- Practice problems on repetition statements: for, while, do…while;
- Usages of continue, break and goto statements;

All these topics are discussed with detailed examples. Further, if needed, there is reference material attached to each topic. To maintain the curiosity and interest of the readers, this unit also provides video links via QR code for the explanation of each topic. At the end of the unit, various types of exercises are provided that include Multiple Choice Questions (MCQs), output-based questions, practical exercises, etc. Moreover, a list of references and suggested readings are given at the end of the unit.

RATIONALE

We begin this unit by explaining the need for control statements in a programming language. We describe the types of control statements. Next, the syntax and semantics of different types of selection statements are discussed, which are used for solving a computational problem. Next, it describes the various repetition statements and their syntax and semantics. We explain the selection and repetition statements using flowcharts for a better understanding. It also explains the unconditional statements used in a programming language. Through this unit, we answer three fundamental questions:

1. How and when to use various selection statements in the C programming language?
2. How to use loops to execute the specific statements repeatedly?
3. How to collectively use selection and repetition statements to solve a real-world problem?

PRE-REQUISITES

Basic Mathematics, Unit-I and II

UNIT OUTCOMES

List of outcomes of this unit is as follows:

U3-O1: Describe the need for control statements in problem-solving using C

U3-O2: Describe types of control statements

U3-O3: Explain syntax and semantics of selection statements

U3-O4: Explain the syntax and semantics of looping statements

U3-O5: Apply selection and looping statements in problem-solving using C

Unit-3 Outcomes	EXPECTED MAPPING WITH COURSE OUTCOMES (1- Weak Correlation; 2- Medium correlation; 3- Strong Correlation)					
	CO-1	CO-2	CO-3	CO-4	CO-5	CO-6
U3-O1	–	3	2	3	–	–
U3-O2	1	3	2	2	–	–
U3-O3	2	2	3	2	–	1
U3-O4	2	2	3	2	–	1
U3-O5	2	2	3	2	–	3

3.1 INTRODUCTION

In previous units, we learned that computer programming helps us to solve real-world problems. To solve a problem, the programmer must have a complete understanding and a planned approach (an algorithm). An algorithm requires a sequence of steps (actions) to be executed in a specific order. Consider the following example.

> ***Example:*** We want to compute the average temperature of the working days from Monday to Friday of a month. To solve this problem, we need to record the temperature of all the working days of the month. Then, compute the average temperature and display it to the user.

The whole process can be done in the following steps:

1. Take a week-day as input from the user,
2. Check whether the week-day is a working day or not,
3. If it is a working day, then record the temperature; otherwise, check for the following condition i.e.
   3.1. If the month is completed (following condition) is true, compute the average temperature and display it.
   3.2. If the condition becomes false, go to the next weekday.
4. Process continues for the number of days in a month.

A graphical representation of the above steps is shown in Fig. 3.1. The diamond-shaped symbol is a decision-making statement, also known as a control statement that transfers the control from one statement to another (it may not be a sequential statement). In this Unit, we'll study various control statements in the C programming language.

> ***Note:*** This graphical representation is also known as flowchart. It depicts the flow of computer programs using various symbols. Please read the ***Know More*** section for more details about the flowchart.

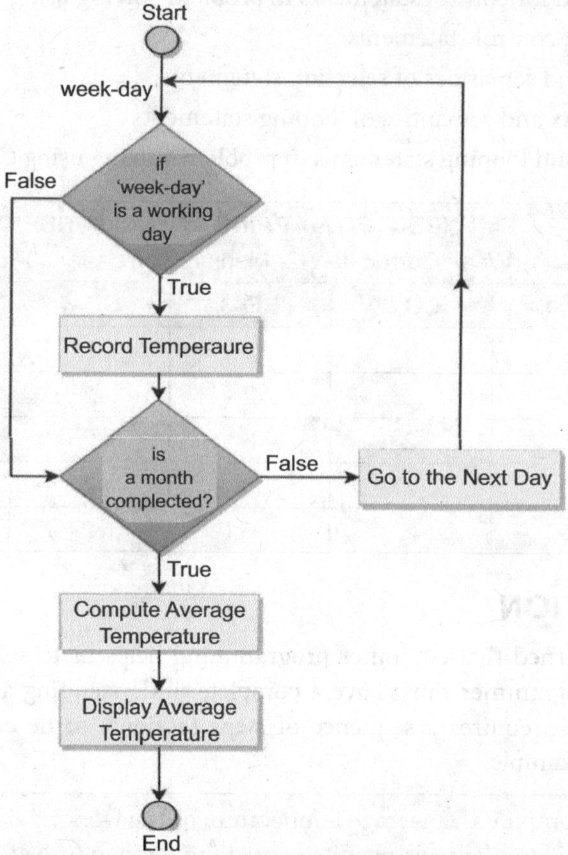

Fig. 3.1: Flowchart of computing the average temperature of all the working days of a month

3.2 CONTROL STATEMENTS

Generally, statements written in a C program execute in sequential order (sequence in which statements have been written). But, certain C statements do not allow sequential execution; instead, they transfer the control to execute statement (other than the one in sequence). This is known as a transfer of control.

There are two types of control statements in the C programming language.

1. Selection statements: `if`, `if..else`, `switch`
2. Repetition statements: `for`, `while`, `do..while`

It is to be noted that, in this unit, the word 'statements' and 'instructions' are used interchangeably and conveys the same meaning. The types of control statements are shown in Fig. 3.2.

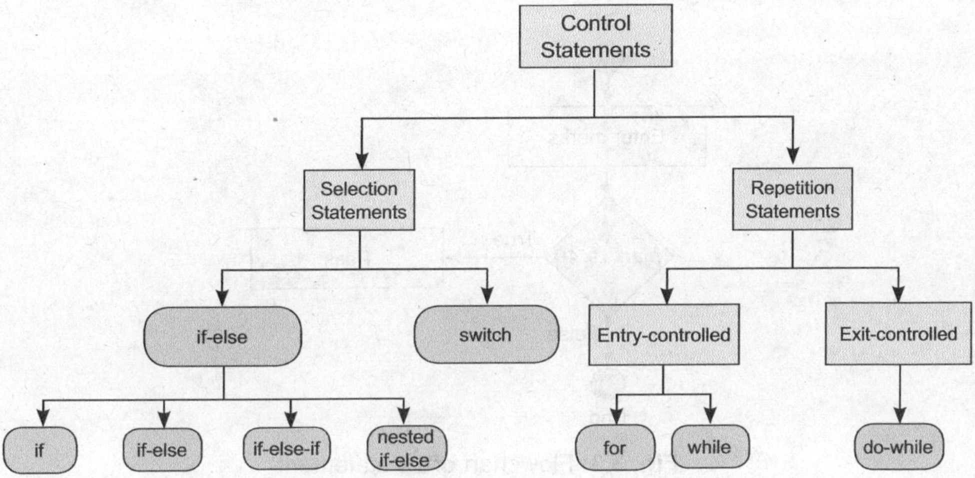

Fig. 3.2: Types of control statements

3.3 SELECTION STATEMENT

In real life, there are times when we make choices, and then we determine what to do next based on those choices. Similar scenarios can occur while programming where we must make choices and execute the following code block based on the choice made. The C language provides two kinds of selection structures. These are as follows, `if-else` statement and `switch` statement. These are also known as decision-making statements. These statements decide the sequence of program execution. The `if-else` statement is further classified as the `if` statement, `if-else` statement, `if-else-if` statement, and nested `if-else` statement, as shown in Fig. 3.2.

3.3.1 The `if` Statement

It is a conditional statement that chooses a statement or a set of statements (action) to execute when the condition becomes true; otherwise, it skips the action. It is the simplest decision-making statement supported by a programming language. The `if` statement is responsible for selecting or skipping a single action. For example, a student passes if he scores more than equal to `40` marks in an examination. Check whether a student passed an examination.

It can be solved using a single if statement as it consists of a single action (decision). A flowchart illustrating the `if` statement is shown in Fig. 3.3. A diamond symbol in a flowchart is used to represent a decision. The decision symbol contains an expression that can either be true or false. If an expression results in zero, it is considered false, and if it results in a non-zero value, it is considered true. The flowchart starts and ends with an oval symbol.

The syntax of the `if` statement is given below.

```
if (expression )
{
   set of statements; // statements executes when the expression evaluates to true.
}
```

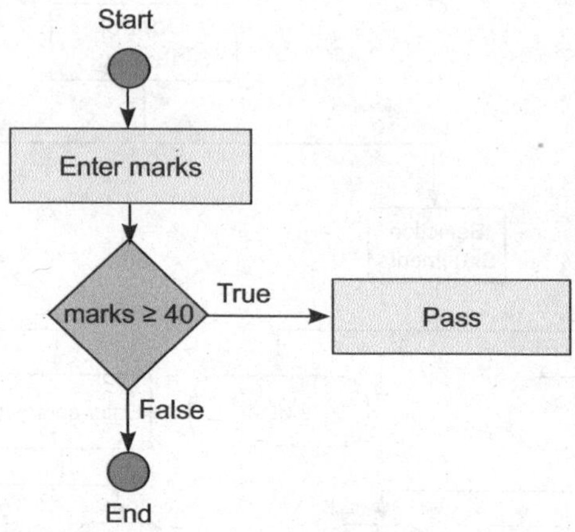

Fig. 3.3: Flowchart of `if` statement

The `if` statement expression results in a boolean value. It could be either true or false. If the expression becomes true, then the body of the `if` statement executes; otherwise not. The open brace { (line 2) and close brace } (line 4) marks the beginning and end of the body of the `if` statement. These braces are required when the body of `if` contains more than one statement to be executed. If these braces are not provided, the first statement after the `if` expression is considered its body. An example of `if` statement is shown in Fig. 3.4.

```
1. #include<stdio.h>
2. int main()
3. {
4.   int marks;
5.   printf(Enter marks);
6.   scanf("%d",&marks);
7.   if(marks >= 40)
8.      printf("You have passed an examination");
9. }
```

Fig. 3.4: Demonstration of the `if` statement

Output:

```
Enter marks 50
You have passed an examination
```

****Note:*** It is assumed that the user enters 50 as an input

```
if(expression)
statement1;
statement2;
statement3;
```

Fig. 3.5: Interpretation of `if` statement

Fig. 3.5 shows the interpretation of `if` statement. If the expression evaluates to true, then only statement1 will be considered as the body of the `if` statement and executes it; otherwise, skips it. statement2 and statement3 are not a part of `if` statement body. So, they get executed in both scenarios if the expression evaluates to true or false.

```
1. if (var1 == 10)
      printf(" value is 10");
2. if(var1 == 10)
      {
       printf(" value is 10 ");
      }
```

Note: Both 1 and 2 are correct and output the same result. But programmers like to keep the code short and clear. So, they prefer 1 (without braces) to write the body if it contains only a single statement.

3.3.2 The if-else Statement

It is a conditional statement that chooses a statement or a set of statements (action) to execute when the condition becomes true; otherwise, it executes another set of statements (action). The `if-else` statement selects one of the two actions. For example, a student passes if he scores more than equal to `40` marks in an examination. Check whether a student passed or failed an examination.

The `if-else` statement checks the condition and performs some actions based on whether the condition gets true or false. A flowchart is shown in Fig. 3.6. We can see that a decision symbol contains an expression that can evaluate as true or false. If it is true, "You have passed an examination" is printed; otherwise, "You have failed an examination" is printed.

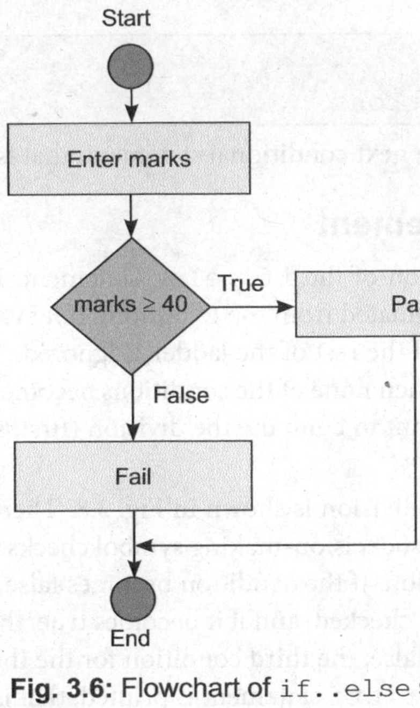

Fig. 3.6: Flowchart of `if..else` statement

The syntax of the `if..else` statement is shown below:

```
if (expression)
{
    set of statements; //statements executes when the expression evaluates to true
}
else
{
    set of statements;//statement executes when the expression evaluates to false
}
```

Here, we can see that there is no condition associated with the else statement. These statements execute only if the condition gets false. An example of the `if..else` statement is shown in Fig 3.7.

```
int main()
{
  int marks;
  printf(Enter marks);
  scanf("%d",&marks);
  if(marks >= 40)
        printf("You have passed an examination");
  else
       printf("You have failed an examination"); }
```

Fig. 3.7: Demonstration of `if..else` statement

Output:

```
Enter marks 35
You have failed an examination
```

Now, we'll head toward learning the next conditional statement, that is, `if-else-if`.

3.3.3 The `if-else-if` Statement

This conditional statement is an extension of the `if..else` statement. It is also known as the `if-else-if` ladder. Here, expression is evaluated from top to bottom. If it evaluates to true, then the body related to the expression is executed, and the rest of the ladder is ignored. The last else statement is the default statement, which gets executed when none of the conditions becomes true. It is used for checking multiple conditions. For example, we want to compute the division (first, second and third) according to the marks earned by a student.

The flowchart for computing the division is shown in Fig. 3.8. There are three decision-making symbols present in the flowchart. The first decision-making symbol checks if the marks are greater than or equal to `60`, then it prints 'First Division'. If the condition becomes false, the next expression written in the second decision-making symbol is checked, and if it becomes true, the second division is printed. Again, if the second condition becomes false, the third condition for the third division is checked. If all of the condition becomes false, the last `printf` statement is printed, that is, fail.

Note: The functioning of the conditional operator (? :), studied in Unit II, is the same as the `if..else` statement. Could you try writing the same code using the ternary operator?

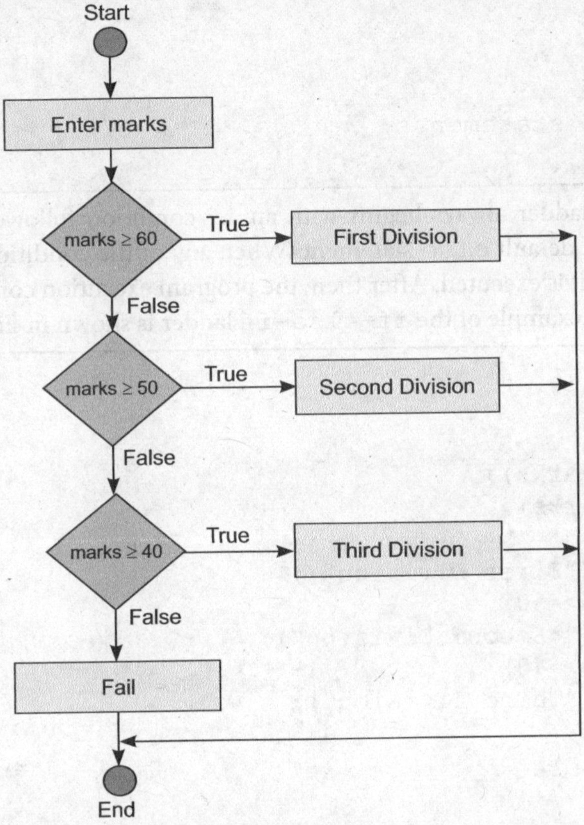

Fig. 3.8: Flowchart of `if-else-if` statement

The syntax of the `if-else-if` statement is shown below:

```
if (expression)
    {
        set of statements;
    }
else if (expression)
    {
       set of statements;
    }
else if (expression)
       {
     set of statements;
    }
```

```
    .
    .
    .
    else
      {
         set of statements;
      }
```

The `if-else-if` ladder always begins with an `if` condition followed by multiple `else if` condition and ends with a default `else` statement. When any of the conditions get true, the `printf` statement associated with it is executed. After then, the program execution comes to an end by skipping the last else statement. An example of the `if-else-if` ladder is shown in Fig. 3.9.

```
int main()
{
 int marks;
 printf(Enter marks);
 scanf("%d",&marks);
 if (marks>=60)
          printf("First Division");
 else if (marks>=50)
          printf(" Second Division");
 else if (marks>=40)
          printf("Third Division");
  else
  printf("Fail");
}
```

Fig. 3.9: Demonstration of `if-else-if` statement

Output:

```
Enter marks 67
67
First Division
```

Now, we'll discuss the last conditional statement, which is a nested `if-else` statement.

3.3.4 The Nested `if-else` Statement

Nesting is defined as adding various `if-else` statements in a body of `if` and `else`. It is used to check a condition within a condition. The nested `if-else` statement places an if statement inside another if statement. For example, check whether a student passes or fails an examination and calculate the division by which he passes an examination.

The flowchart is shown in Fig. 3.10. We can see that the first decision-making symbol is checking whether a student passed an exam or not. If he passes, the control goes to the next decision-making statement, computing whether a student earned first division or not. If yes, it prints the first division; otherwise, it will check for the third decision-making statement that checks for the second division. If yes, it prints the second division; otherwise, it will check for the last decision-making statement, which checks for the third division.

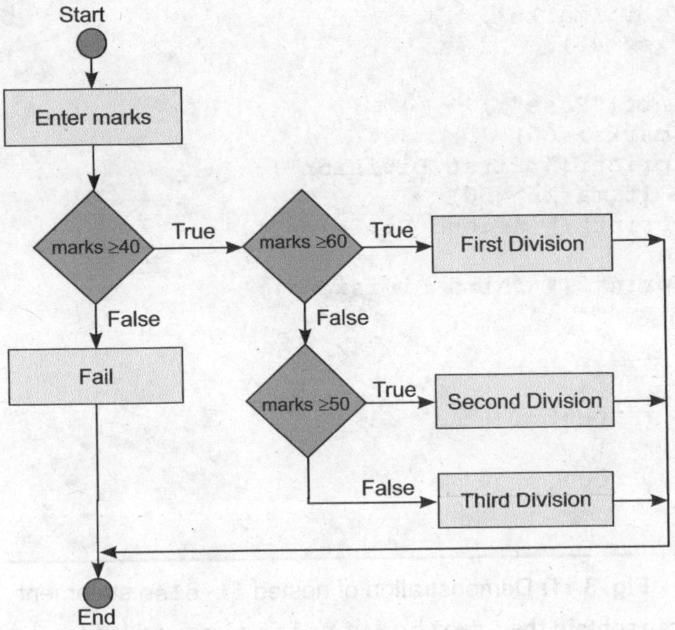

Fig. 3.10: Flowchart of nested `if-else` statement

The syntax of the nested `if-else` statement is shown below:

```
if (expression)
{
        //enters the body when the expression evaluates to true
   if (expression)
    {
        statements;  // executes statements when the second expression evaluates to true.
    }
    else
    {
        statements;  // executes statements when the second expression evaluates to false.
    }
}
    else
    {
        statements;
    }
```

```
#include<stdio.h>
int main() {
     int marks;
     printf("Enter marks");
     scanf("&d",&marks);
     if (marks>=40)
     {
          printf("Pass");
          if(marks>=60)
              printf(" First Division");
        else if(marks>=50)
              printf(" Second Division");
          else
              printf(" Third Division");
  }
  else
  {
     printf("Fail");
  }

     return 0;
}
```

Fig. 3.11: Demonstration of nested `if-else` statement

The body of `if` can contain the `if`, `else-if` or `if-else-if` ladder and the body of `else` can also contain `if-else` statements. It is important to remember that only one block executes either `if` or `else`, depending on the conditions. When `if` block executes, the `else` block is skipped and vice versa.

Output:

```
Enter marks 77
First Division
```

An example of a nested `if-else` statement is shown in Fig. 3.11. If a student passes the examination, the control goes into the `if's` body and computes the division based on earned marks; otherwise, it executes the `else's` body, and prints Fail. The next decision-making symbol inside its body checks for a student's division. Here, we used the `if-else-if` ladder to check the student's division. So, if the `if` condition gets true, the associated `printf` statement executes otherwise, control goes to the `else if` condition and checks it for the second division. If this condition gets true, 'Second Division' is printed; otherwise, the body of `else` executes and prints Third Division.

Scan QR code for Answer

Question 3.1: What happens when there are multiple if statements and a single else statement in a program?

The compiler might get confused about to which if-statement the else part belongs. This is known as the dangling else problem, shown in Fig. 3.12. The problem arises when one else statement corresponds to multiple if statements. The else becomes dangling else. It occurs only in nested if-else statements. In such cases, the else clause belongs to the innermost if statement.

```
if (expression)
        if (expression)
             if (expression)
     else
        printf("else associates with the innermost if statement");
```

Fig. 3.12: Demonstration of dangling else

However, the else can become part of another if statement by enclosing it within braces. In Fig. 3.13, the else clause is the part of the outermost if statement.

```
if (expression){
        if (expression)
             if (expression)
   }
   else
        printf("else associates with the outermost if statement");
```

Fig. 3.13: Demonstration of dangling else

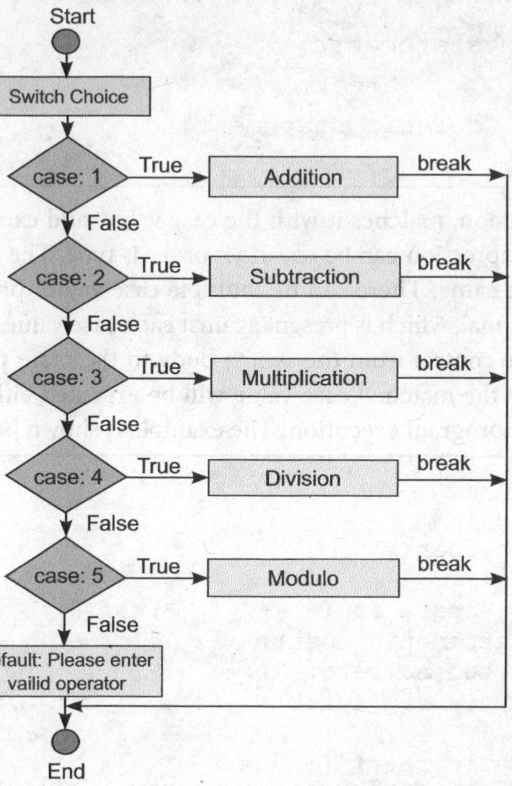

Fig. 3.14: Flowchart of the `switch` statement

3.3.5 The `switch` Statement

This statement is an alternative to the `if-else-if` ladder. It is used for executing multiple operations against the evaluated value of an expression. For example, Design a calculator to perform basic arithmetic operations by taking two numbers from the user.

The flowchart is shown in Fig. 3.14. It takes two numbers from the user and displays all the arithmetic operations; then, a user chooses one of the operations to be performed on the numbers. The operation that a user chooses matches the different case values. If it matches, the operation associated with the case is performed; otherwise, it matches with the next case value. The default case is executed if it doesn't match any of the cases.

The syntax of the `switch` statement is shown below:

```
switch(expression)
{
case value 1:    statements;
                         break;
case value 2:    statements;
                         break;
...
...
case value n:    statements;
                         break;
   default:      default statement;
   }
```

It evaluates the expression, matches it with the case value, and executes the statements associated with that case value. The expression can be of `char` or `int` type. The type of expression and the case value should always be the same. There can be multiple case values present in a `switch` statement. The break statement is optional, which is present against each case value. It terminates the switch block's execution and transfers the control from the switch body to the main program. If it is not present, all the statements followed by the matched case value will be executed either until it encounters. a break statement or completes the program execution. The example is shown below in Fig. 3.15.

```
#include<stdio.h>
int main() {
   char arthmetic_oper;
   int var1, var2;
   printf("Select operator (+, -, /, *,%): ");
   scanf("%c", &arthmetic_oper);
   printf("Enter two numbers: ");
   scanf("%d %d", &var1, &var2);

   switch (arthmetic_oper) {
     case '+':  printf("Addition is %d",var1 + var2);
                break;
```

```
    case '-':  printf("Subtraction is %d",var1 - var2);
               break;
    case '/':  printf("Division is %d",var1 / var2);
               break;
    case '*':  printf("Multiplication is %d",var1 * var2);
               break;
    case '%':  printf("Modulus is %d",var1 % var2);
               break;
    // if arthmetic_oper does not match with any of the operators, then the default case executes
    default :  printf("Please enter valid operator");
  }

  return 0;
}
```

Fig. 3.15: Demonstration of `switch` statement

Output:

```
Select operator (+, -, /, *,%): *
Enter two numbers: 23 34
Multiplication is 782
```

***Note:** It is assumed that the user enters 23 and 34 as an input

Question 3.2: Can you try solving the same example we took for the if-else-if ladder using the switch statement?

Next, we'll discuss the second type of control statement, repetition statements, in the following section.

3.4 REPETITION STATEMENT

Let us consider a listener who wants to listen to several songs. For that, he has two ways:

First way: The listener can play the songs one by one, in which he has to play a new song by himself every time the old one is over.

Second way: The listener adds all selected songs to a playlist, and a player plays the songs one by one. After finishing the old song, the player runs a new song; this process repeats until the playlist is not finished. The listener can listen to his complete playlist without bothering to play songs repeatedly. The flowchart shows the process of second way of playing the songs using the loop shown in Fig. 3.16.

In the C programming language, repetition statements are also known as looping or iteration statements.

Loop is used to perform the same task repeatedly. Every loop has its body which consists of several instructions to perform a specific task. The loop's body starts from the { and end with the }. The loop iterates the number of statements written inside it until the condition is not false. The loop is known as **finite** if it stops executing after a specific iteration. A loop is **infinite** if it continues to execute the statements written inside its body. The main advantage of the loop is that it reduces the size of the code.

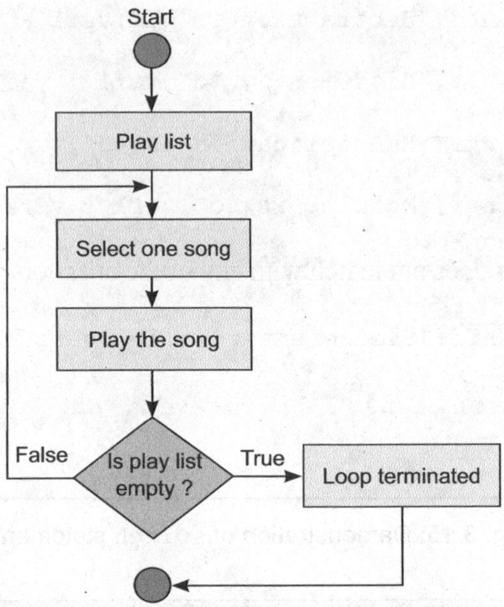

Fig. 3.16: Flowchart to play song play list

The execution condition controls the execution of the loop. Based on the execution condition, the loop is divided into two types:

1. Entry control loop
   (a) `while` loop (b) `for` loop
2. Exit control loop
   (a) `do-while` loop

3.4.1 Entry Control Loop

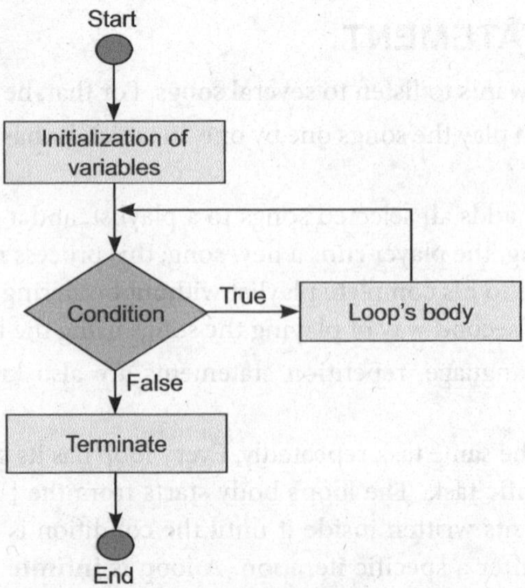

Fig. 3.17: Flowchart of `while` loop

The loop which checks the condition first before executing the loop's body is known as the entry control loop. The `while` and `for` loops are the entry control loop.

`while` loop. The `while` loop is the type of entry control loop. In this loop, first, the condition is checked, and if the condition is true, then statements written inside the loop will be executed otherwise, the loop will be terminated. The flowchart of the `while` loop is shown in Fig. 3.17.

Syntax of `while` loop

```
Initialization;
while(condition)
{
    instructions;
    Variable updating statement (Increment/Decrement);
}
```

Steps involved in the `while` loop:

Step 1: This is the initializing step. Here value will initialize to the loop variable.

Step 2: The `while` loop checks the condition. If the condition is true, the loop's body will execute; otherwise, the loop will terminate.

Step 3: The statements written inside the body will execute. Also, the variable's value will update and return to the condition check.

Step 4: The body of the while loop will execute until the condition is not false. The loop will terminate when the condition is false, and the statements written after the loop will execute.

Example: Suppose we want to print the number from 0 to 4; this can be done using the loop, shown in Fig 3.18.

```
/*Program to print numbers from 0 to 4 using while loop*/
1. #include <stdio.h>
2. int main()
3. {
4.      int var1;
5.      var1=0;                    // Initialization of the loop's variable
6.      while(var1<5)              // Checking condition
7.      {
8.          printf("var1= %d\n",var1);
9.          var1++;                // Updating loop's variable
10.     }
11.return 0;
12. }
```

Fig. 3.18: Program to print numbers from 0 to 4 using a `while` loop

The above example prints 0 to 5 numbers on the output screen. In this, line 5 initializes the loop variable (var1). Line 6 is the entrance of the `while` loop, where it checks the condition. If the condition is true, it returns 1, and the loop's body will execute. In line 9, value of the variable will update, and control of the loop will go back to line 6. This process will continue until the condition is not false. The output of the given an example shown is below.

Output:

```
var1= 0
var1= 1
var1= 2
var1= 3
var1= 4
```

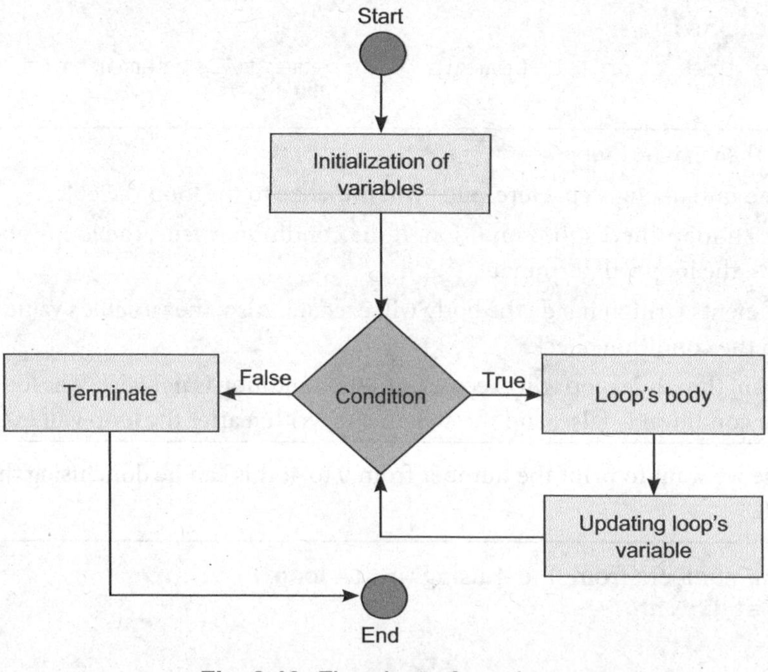

Fig. 3.19: Flowchart of `for` loop

`for` loop. The `for` loop is also a type of entry control loop. It is the most popular loop structure. This loop checks the condition before executing the body. If the condition is true, then the loop's body will execute. If the condition is false, then the loop terminates. The flowchart of the `for` loop is shown in Fig. 3.19.

Syntax of the `for` loop

```
for( Initialization ; Condition ; Updation)
{
   Instructions   // body of the loop
}
```

The `for` loop is divided into three blocks apart from the body: initialization, condition, and updation. Each part is separated by the semicolons (`;`).

Steps involved in execution of the `for` loop:

Step 1: The execution of the loop starts from the initialization part that initializes the loop variable. This part executes only one time.

Step 2: After the initialization part, the condition part will execute. If the condition is true, then the control of the loop will go inside the loop's body.

Step 3: The loop's body contains multiple instructions to perform a specific task. The loop's body will execute when the condition block returns 1 (true). After executing the loop's body, control will transfer to the updation block.

Step 4: In the updation block loop's variable will update, and the control goes to the condition block. This process will continue until the condition is not false.

Example: Suppose we want to print the number from 0 to 4; this can be done using the `for` loop, shown in Fig 3.20.

```
/*Program to print number from 0 to 4 using for loop*/
1. #include <stdio.h>
2. int main()
3. {
4.      int var1;
5.         for(var1=0; var1<5; var1++)
7.      {
8.           printf("var1= %d\n",var1);
9.      }
10.return 0;
11.  }
```

Fig. 3.20: Program to print numbers from 0 to 4 using a `for` loop

Output:

```
var1= 0
var1= 1
var1= 2
var1= 3
var1= 4
```

The above example prints numbers from 0 to 4 using the `for` loop. Here in line 5, we use the `for` loop. The initialization, condition, and variable updating are done in their respective parts in the `for` loop. The initialization part initializes the variable `var1` by 0; it is executed only once and at the start of the loop. Next, the condition `var1<5` executes, and if it is true, the loop's body executes. In the end, updation block will execute, which increases the value of `var1` by 1 `(var1++)`. The flow of `for` loop (condition→ loop's body → updation→condition) will continue until the condition block is not false.

Note:

- The `for` loop can be written with empty initialization, condition, or updation blocks. If the `for` loop is written without any condition, then that loop is an infinite loop.

Example:

```
for( ;  ; )
{
   printf("Without condition\n");
}
```

Following code print `Without condition` infinite times.

- If we put a semicolon (`;`) after the for loop, the loop becomes a single-line statement. It means the loop will execute properly, but all the statements written inside the body will be treated outside the loop and will not execute repeatedly.

Example:

```
for (int var1=0; var1<5; var1++);
{
   printf("loop with a semicolon\n");
}
```

The following code will print `loop with a semicolon` once, but the value of `var1` will be 5 after executing the loop. Because the loop will execute until the condition is not false, but due to the semicolon, it becomes a single line statement and does not execute the loop body.

3.4.2 Exit Control Loop

The loop that checks the condition after executing the loop body is known as the exit control loop. The `do-while` loop is the exit control loop.

`do-while` loop

This loop first executes the loop's body and then checks the condition. If the condition is true, the loop body is executed again; otherwise the loop terminates. The body of `do-while` loop executes at least once because the loop control condition is checked at the end of the loop's body. The flow of the `do-while` loop is shown in Fig 3.21.

Syntax of the `do-while` loop

```
Initialization;
do
{
     Instructions;          //body of the loop
     Updation;            //increment/decrement operations
}while(condition);
```

Steps involved in the execution of the `do-while` loop:

Step 1: Initialize the loop's variables before executing the loop.

Step 2: Loop starts from the `do` keyword; first, the loop's body will execute.

Step 3: Loop's variables are updated inside the body.

Step 4: The condition for the loop control is written inside the `while`, which executes after the loop's body. If the condition is true, the loop's body will execute again; otherwise, the loop will terminate.

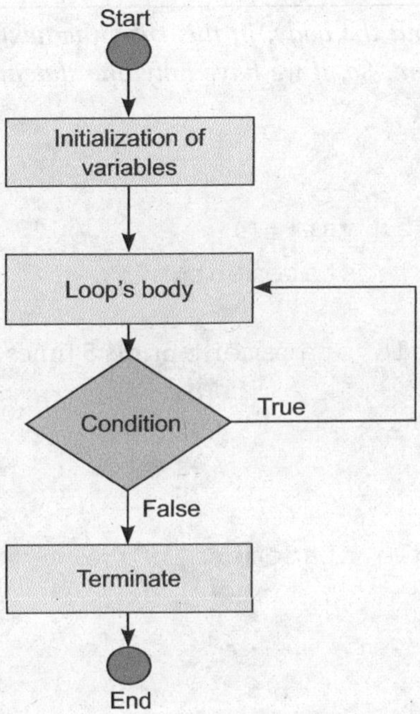

Fig. 3.21: Flowchart of the `do-while` loop

/*Program to print number from 0 to 4 using do-while loop*/

```
#include <stdio.h>
int main()
{
  int var1;
  var1=0;        // Initialization of the loop's variable
  do             // starting of do-while loop
  {
    printf("var1= %d\n",var1);
    var1++;              // Updating variable
  }while(var1<5);     // Checked condition
  return 0;
  }
```

Fig. 3.22: Program to print numbers from 0 to 4 using a `do-while` loop

Output:

```
var1= 0
var1= 1
var1= 2
var1= 3
var1= 4
```

> ***Note:*** *We can write a loop without the body; in this case, the next statement written after the loop is considered the loop body statement. So, if we have only one statement inside the loop, we can write it without the body.*
>
> Example:
>
> ```
> for (int var1=0; var1<5; var1++)
> printf("loop with single statement\n");
> ```
>
> In this case, `loop with single statement` prints 5 times
>
> Similarly,
>
> ```
> while(var1==0)
> printf("loop with single statement\n");
> ```
>
> and
>
> ```
> do
> printf("loop with single statement\n");
> while(var1==0);
> ```

The example shown in Fig 3.22 prints numbers from `0` to `4` using the `do-while` loop. Here loop's variable initializes at line 5. The body of the loop will start after the do keyword. Thus, first, the body will execute and print the variable `var1` value on the screen. In line 9, the value of the `var1` will be incremented by `1`, and it also marks the end of `do-while` loop. After that condition written inside the while executes. If the condition is true, the loop's body will execute again; otherwise, the loop will terminate.

break and continue statements

The `break` and `continue` are the statements used to control the loops. They both are unconditional statements.

break statement

The `break` statement is used for two purposes in `C` language. First, it stops the execution of the `case` in a `switch` statement. Second, it stops the current execution and send the control outside the loop. So, whenever the `break` statement executes, it terminates the current loop and sends the control or flow of the program just after the loop.

Syntax

```
break;
```

Example: Here, we extend the previous example (shown in Fig 3.22). In this, we terminate the loop using the break statement whenever the value of `var1` reaches 3, shown in Fig 3.23.

```
/*Program to print numbers from 0 to 4 using for loop*/
#include <stdio.h>
int main()
{
      int var1;
        for(var1=0; var1<5; var1++)
      {
          if(var1==3)
            break;
          printf("var1= %d\n",var1);
      }
      return 0;
}
```

Fig. 3.23: Demonstration of the `break` statement

In the above example, we used a `break` statement inside the `if`. Therefore, when the `if` statement condition is true, the `break` will execute. The `break` statement terminates the loop and sends the control outside the loop. In above example, *specifically, when* `var1` *is at* 3, *the condition of* `if` will be true, the `break` will execute, and the loop will terminate. That's why 3 will not print on the output screen.

Output

```
var1= 0
var1= 1
var1= 2
```

`continue` statement

The `continue` statement is used to skip the current iteration in the loop. Whenever the `continue` statement executes, it interrupts the flow of the loop and sends the control to the end of the body (`}`) for the current iteration only. So, the statements written after the `continue` statement will not be executed.

Syntax

```
continue;
```

Example: Here, we update the previous example (Fig 3.23). In this, we write a program to skip the value of 2 when the program prints numbers from 0 to 4, shown in Fig 3.24.

```
/*Program to print number from 0 to 4 using for loop*/
#include <stdio.h>
int main()
{
      int var1;
        for(var1=0; var1<5; var1++)
      {
          if(var1==2)
            continue;
          printf("var1= %d\n",var1);
      }
      return 0;
}
```

Fig. 3.24: Demonstration of the `continue` statement

In the above example, we used a `continue` statement inside the `if`. When `var1` is at `2`, the condition of `if` will return true, the `continue` statement will execute, and the control of the loop will be transferred to the end of the body. After that, the variable's value will update (from `2` to `3`) in the updation block, and the next iteration will start. That's why `2` will not print on the output screen.

Output

```
var1= 0
var1= 1
var1= 3
var1= 4
```

Another example is to check given number is a prime number or not is given in Fig 3.25. It takes an integer number from the user to check the prime number in line 5. In line 6, we initialize a `mark` variable with a `0` value. This variable is used to verify that the given number is divided by the other than itself and `1` or not; if yes, then at line 11, we update it with `1` and terminate the loop using the `break` statement. After executing the loop, we check the status of the `mark` variable. If it remains `0`, the given number is not divisible by other numbers except by itself and `1`, and the message `The given number is a prime number` will print on the screen. Otherwise, it will print that `The given number is not a prime number`.

```
1. #include <stdio.h>
2. int main() {
3.   int var1, mark;
4.   printf("Enter the integer number to check the prime number ");
5.   scanf("%d",&var1);

6.   mark=0;
7.   for(int itr=2; itr<var1; itr++)
8.   {
9.        if(var1%itr==0)
10.       {
11.           mark=1;
12.           break;
13.       }
14.  }
15.  if(mark==1)
16.       printf("The given number is not a prime number");
17.  else
18.       printf("The given number is a prime number");
     return 0;
19. }
```

Fig. 3.25: Example to check prime number

Output

```
Enter the integer number to check the prime number 11
The given number is a prime number
```

***Note:** It is assumed that the user enters 11 as an input

Another example: suppose we want to design a calculator which will perform arithmetic operations until the user does not say exit. Here we follow some simple steps to create such a type of calculator:

1. Design a calculator that performs the simple arithmetic task. (This can be done using the switch statement, as we have already done in Fig 3.15)
2. Next, put the switch statement inside the loop.

```
1.   #include<stdio.h>
2.   int main() {
3.     char arthmetic_oper;
4.     char che;
5.     int var1, var2;

6.   do
7.   {
8.     printf("Select operator (+, -, /, *, %): ");
9.     scanf("%c", &arthmetic_oper);
10.    printf("Enter two numbers: ");
11.    scanf("%d %d", &var1, &var2);

12.    switch (arthmetic_oper) {
13.      case '+':  printf("Addition is %d",var1 + var2);
14.                 break;
15.      case '-':  printf("Subtraction is %d",var1 - var2);
16.                 break;
17.      case '/':  printf("Division is %d",var1 / var2);
18.                 break;
19.      case '*':  printf("Multiplication is %d",var1 * var2);
20.                 break;
21.      case '%':  printf("Modulus is %d",var1 % var2);
22.                 break;
// if arthmetic_oper does not match with any of the operators, then the default case executes
23.      default :  printf("Please enter valid operation");
24.      }

25.      printf("\nFor the continue enter y or Y\n");
26.      scanf("%c", &che);
27.     }while(che=='y'||che=='Y');
28.    printf("Calculator terminated");
29.    return 0;
30.  }
```

Fig. 3.26: Calculator using the `do-while` loop

In the above example (Fig 3.26), we create a calculator that performs an arithmetic operation. For continuous execution, we put it in the loop. Here we used the `do-while` loop because `do-while` executes the instruction at least once without checking the condition, and we want to perform the arithmetic operation at least once. In lines 25 and 26, it asks the user for a character `'y'` or `'Y'` for the continuation; if the user inputs `'y'` or `'Y'`, then in line 27 condition will be true, and the loop will continue for the next iteration. The loop will be terminated if the user inputs other characters in place of the `'y'` or `'Y'`.

Output:

```
Select operator (+, -, /, *, %): *
Enter two numbers: 23
2
Multiplication is 46
For the continue enter y or Y
y
Select operator (+, -, /, *, %): -
Enter two numbers: 23
45
Subtraction is -22
For the continue enter y or Y
n
Calculator terminated
```

****Note:* It is assumed that the user enters 23 and 2 as an input*

3.4.3 Nested Loop

When one loop is written inside another loop is known as a nested loop. It is also called a loop inside the loop. Any number of loops can be defined inside another loop. The depth of nesting can be `n`. Fig 3.27 shows the flow of the nested loop, where the inner and outer loop can be any loop (`while, for` and `do-while`).

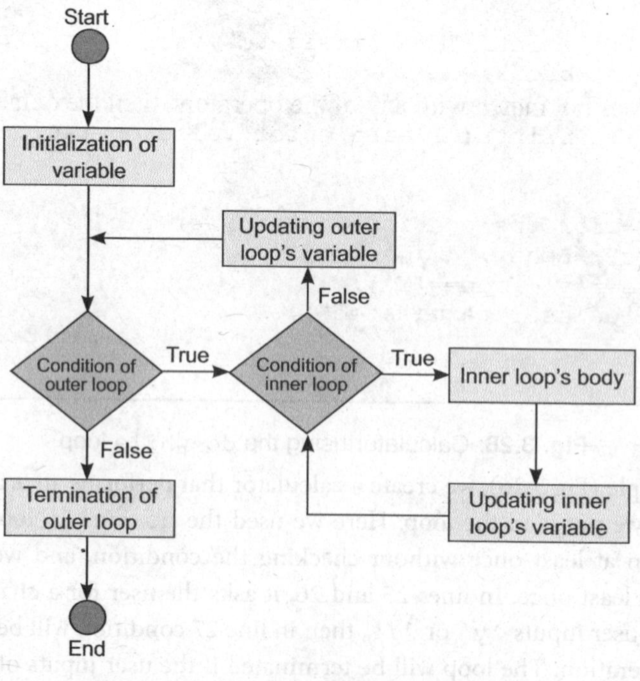

Fig. 3.27: Flow chart of the nested loop

The loop containing another loop is known as the **outer loop**, and the loop written inside the other loop is known as the **inner loop**.

```
Outerloop
{
        Body of the outer loop;
        Innerloop
        {
              Body of the inner loop;
        }
}
```

For a better understanding of the nested loop, let's take the example of printing the prime number between 1 and 50. We used the inner loop (line 8) to check the given number. If the number is a prime number, it will print on the screen (as we have already seen in Fig). The outer loop (line 5) chooses numbers one by one for checking the prime. This loop iterates from 2 to 50 (As we already know that 1 is not the prime number, so we start the outer loop from 2). In every outer loop iteration, the inner loop checks whether the corresponding number is a prime number or not, as shown in Fig 3.28.

```
1.  #include <stdio.h>
2.  int main()
3.  {
4.   int var1, mark, num;
5.   printf("The prime number between 1 to 50 are:\n");
6.   for(num=2; num<=50; num++)              //outer loop
7.   {
8.      mark=0;
9.      for(int itr=2; itr<var1; itr++)   // inner loop
10.     {
11.         if(var1%itr==0)
12.         {
13.           mark=1;
14.           break;
15.         }
16.     }
17.     if(mark==0)
18.        printf("%d",num);
19.   }
20.   return 0;
21. }
```

Fig. 3.28: Demonstration of the nested loop

Output:

```
The prime number between 1 to 50 are
2  3  5  7  11  13  17  19  23  29  31  37  41  43  47
```

Another examples:

Let's take an example to calculate the factorial of the given number.

```
#include <stdio.h>
int main()
{
    int var1,fact_var=1,num_var;
    printf("Enter an integer number: ");
    scanf("%d",&num_var);
    for(var1=1;var1<=num_var;var1++)
    {
      fact_var=fact_var*var1;
    }
    printf("Factorial of %d is: %d",num_var,fact_var);
    return 0;
}
```

Fig. 3.29: Program to calculate the factorial

To calculate the factorial of any number, we have to compute the multiplication of all positive integers less than the number. So here, we start the loop from `1` to `num_var`, where `num_var` is the user-entered number, and perform the multiplication between the loop variable (`var1`) and `fact_var`. The `fact_var` is the variable initialized by `1` and is used to store the product's result in each iteration, shown in Fig 3.29.

Output

```
Enter an integer number: 5
Factorial of 5 is: 120
```

**Note: It is assumed that the user enters 5 as an input*

3.4.4 Goto Statement

It is a jump statement that transfers the program's control from one place to another within the function. The `goto` statement sends the program's control to the specific label already defined in the program. Transferring the control does not depend on the condition that's why it is also known as the unconditional jump statement. The `label` can be defined before or after the `goto` statement. The name of the `label` can also be changed.

Syntax

label:	goto label;
...	...
...	...
goto label;	label:

In the above syntax, `goto` transfers the program control to the specific label after reading the `goto label`.

Example

```
1. #include <stdio.h>
2.
3. int main()
4. {
5.     int var1 = 0;
6.     here:
7.       printf("%d ",var1);
8.       var1++;
9.     if (var1 <= 5)
10.        goto here;
11.    return 0;
12. }
```

Fig. 3.30: Demonstration of the `goto` statement

In the above example (Fig 3.30) defines the label in line 6 as `here`. After the execution of the `goto` statement (at line 10), the control of the execution will transfer at the specified label `here`, which will continue until the `if` statement will not return `false`.

Output:

```
0 1 2 3 4 5
```

UNIT SUMMARY

Introduction

- Generally, statements written in a C program execute in sequential order (sequence in which statements have been written).
- There are certain C statements that do not allow sequential execution; instead, they transfer the control to execute statement (other than the one in sequence). This is known as transfer of control.
- There are two control statements for writing any C program: selection statements and repetition statements.

Selection Statements

- They are also known as decision-making statements as they decide the sequence of program execution.
- These are of two types: if-else and switch statements. The if-else statement is further classified as the if statement, if-else statement, if-else-if statement, and nested if-else statement.
- The if-statement is the simplest decision-making statement and is responsible for selecting or skipping a single action.

- The if-else statement selects one of the two actions. It executes a set of statements when the condition gets true; otherwise, it executes another set of statements.
- The functioning of the if-else statement is the same as the conditional operator (?:) which is a ternary operator.
- If a single statement exists in the if's body, opening and closing braces can be avoided.
- The if-else-if statement is known as the if-else-if ladder. The if-else-if ladder always begins with an if condition followed by multiple else if condition and ends with a default else statement.
- Nesting is defined as adding various if-else statements in a body of if and else. The nested if-else is used to check a condition within a condition.
- The problem of dangling else arises in a nested if-else statement when there is one else statement that corresponds to multiple if statements. In such cases, the else becomes part of the innermost if statement.
- The switch statement is the alternative to the if-else-if ladder. It is used for executing multiple operations against the evaluated value of an expression.
- It evaluates the expression, matches it with the case value, and executes the statements associated with that case value. The expression can be of char or int type.

Repetition Statements

- The repetition statements are used when we repeatedly want to perform the same task (action). Loops are used as repetition statements.
- Every loop has its body which consists of several instructions to perform a specific task. The loop iterates the number of statements written inside it until the condition is not false.
- There are two types of loops: entry-controlled and exit-controlled loops.
- The loop which checks the condition first before executing the sloop's body is known as the entry control loop. The while and for loops are the entry control loop.
- The for and while loop first checks the condition, and if the condition is true, then statements written inside the loop will be executed otherwise, the loop will be terminated.

- The for loop is divided into three blocks apart from the body: initialization, condition, and updation. Each part is separated by the semicolons (;).
- The loop that checks the condition after executing the loop body is known as the exit control loop. The do-while loop is the exit control loop.
- This loop first executes the loop's body and then checks the condition. If the condition is true, the loop body is executed again; otherwise, the loop will be terminated.
- The do-while loop executes at least once because the loop control condition is checked at the end of the loop's body.
- The break and continue are the statements used to control the loops. They both are unconditional statements.
- Break statement is used to stop the execution of the loop and send the control *outside the loop, which executes the* statements written after the loop.
- The continue statement is used to skip the current iteration in the loop. Whenever the continue statement executes, it interrupts the flow of the loop and sends the control to the end of the body for the current iteration only.

EXERCISES

Multiple Choice Questions

1. Suppose the programmer wants to run some instructions using the loop, but he wants to ensure that these instructions should be run at least once. Which loop should he have to use?

(a) for loop (b) do-while loop (c) while loop (d) All of these

2. The continue statement is used in the loop when the programmer wants to __________.

(a) skip the specific statements (b) terminate the loop
(c) interrupt the loop (d) None of these

3. Which unconditional statement is used to shift the program control from one place to another within a function?

(a) do-while (b) if-else (c) while (d) goto

4. Which conditional statement would be useful for making a decision based on multiple choices?

(a) if (b) if-else (c) if-else-if (d) None of these

5. Which keyword is used to handle the unwanted case in the switch?

(a) case (b) break (c) switch (d) default

ANSWERS									
1.	(b)	2.	(a)	3.	(d)	4.	(c)	5.	(d)

Output-based Questions.

(What will be the output of the following programs?)

A

```
#include<stdio.h>
int main()
{
  if(-10)
    printf(«H»);
    printf(«I»);
  else;
    printf(«By»);
    printf(«e»);
  return 0;
}
```

B

```
#include<stdio.h>
int main()
{
 int var1 = 0;
 for (var1=2.6; var1<7.3;
var1++)
 {
   printf(«%d «, var1);
 }
 return 0;
}
```

C

```
#include<stdio.h>
int main()
{
  int var1=3.4;
  switch(var1)
  {
   case 1: printf(" 1");
   case 3: printf("%d ",var1++);
   case 6: printf(" 6");
   default: printf(" Default");
  }
  switch(var1)
  {
   case 1: printf(" 1");
   case 3: printf(" 3");
  case 6: printf(" 6");
  default: printf(" Value");
break;
  }
   return 0;}
```

D

```
#include<stdio.h>
int main()
{
  int var = 97;
  while ( var <= 104 ) {
    printf( «%c», var );
    if ( var % 5 == 0 )
      printf( «\n» );
    else
      printf( «  « );
    var++;
  }
  return 0;
}
```

E

```
#include<stdio.h>
int main()
{
    int var = 97;
    for(var =0; var; var++)
     if(var<3)
       printf(«My Rules «);
    printf(«No Rules «);
    return 0;
}
```

F

```
 #include <stdio.h>
 int main()
 {
    printf("%c ", 65);
    goto level1;
    printf("%c ", 66);
    level1:goto level2;
    printf("%c ", 67);
    level2:printf("%c ", 68);
  }
```

G

```
 #include <stdio.h>
 int main()
 {
   int var1=97;
   for(; var1<101; var1++)
   {
     printf("%d", var1);
     for(int var2=var1;
var2<=var1; var2++)
     {
       printf(": %c, ", var2);
     }
   }
   return 0;
 }
```

H

```
#include <stdio.h>
int main()
{
  int var1 = 1, var = 0;
  while(printf(«%d «,var1--)&&
var<5)
  {
    if (var1==0)
      var++;
      var1++;
   }
   printf(«%d «, var1+var);
  return 0;
}
```

I

```
#include<stdio.h>
int main()
{
  int p;
  if(p=3,4,5,6)
    printf(«Computer «);
  else
    printf(« Programming»);
  printf(«%d\n»,p);
  return 0;
}
```

J

```
#include<stdio.h>
int main()
{
  int p = 1, q = -1, r = 0, s;
  s = ++p && ++q || r -;
  if(s)
    printf("Computer \n");
  else if(r)
    printf("Programming \n");
  else
    printf("Computer
Programming \n");
  return 0;
 }
```

Answers of Output-based Questions	
A. Compile-time error	B. 2 3 4 5 6 7
C. 3 6 Default Value	D. a b c d e f g h
E. No Rules	F. A D
G. 97: a, 98: b, 99: c, 100: d,	H. 1 1 1 1 1 1 5
I. Computer 3	J. Programming

Short and Long Answer Type Questions

1. Replace the statements with the code which can print the following output

   for (var1=0; var1<50; var++)

   { statements; }

   (a) 5 10 15 20 25
   (b) 2 3 5 7 11 13 17
   (c) 0 3 6 9 12 15 18 21
   (d) 1 11 21 31 41

2. Fill in the blanks

   (a) In the switch statement, the ____________will run when the entered choice in switch statement does not match with any of the cases.
   (b) The ____________ loop is used when we need to execute specific statements at least once.
   (c) In a `for` loop if the condition block is empty then the loop will be ____________.
   (d) The __________ statements are also known as the unconditional jump statement. They can shift the control of the program from anywhere to anywhere within the function.
   (e) The __________ statement is used to exit from the loop or the switch statement at a specific condition.

Answers			
(a) default	(b) do-while	(c) infinite	(d) goto
(e) break			

3. The following are incomplete programs along with their outputs. Complete the programs by writing the appropriate code to get the desired output.

A

```
#include<stdio.h>
int main()
{
    for(int var1=0;var1<5;var1++)
    {
        printf(«I love «);
        ____________;                    // Fill in the blanks
    }
```

```
    printf(«Programming»);
        return 0;
  }
Output: I love Programming
```

B

```
#include<stdio.h>
int main()
{
    switch(2)
    {
    case 1:
         printf(«No «);

    case 2:
         printf(«%s»,»I Love «);
         goto prog;

    case 3:
         printf(«Coding «);

    case 4:____________                   // Fill in the blanks
         printf(«Programming «);
    }
    return 0;
}
Output: I Love Programming
```

C

```
#include<stdio.h>
int main()
{
  for(int var1=0;var1<5;var1++)
  {
    for(int var2=______; var2<5; var2++)  // Fill in the blanks
        printf(«*»);
    printf(«______”);
  }
    return 0;
```

```
11.    }
Output:
*****
****
***
**
*
```

D

```
1. #include<stdio.h>
2. int main()
3. {
4.       int var1=________;                              // Fill in the blanks
5.       ______{                                  // Fill in the blanks
6.             printf(«Repeat «);
7.             var1--;
8.       }while(var1!=0);
9.
10.         return 0;
11.    }
Output: Repeat Repeat
```

Answers		
(a) Line 7: break	(b) Line 13: prog:	(c) Line 6: var1 and line 8: \n
(d) Line 4: 2 and line 5: do		

PRACTICAL

1. Write a program to ask the user to enter an integer number and perform the following operations:
   (a) Count the total number of digits present in a number.
   (b) Count the sum of event digits of the number.
   (c) Count the sum of odd digits of the number.
   (d) Count the sum and average of all the digits of a number.
2. Write a program using nested if-else to find whether an entered number is negative, positive or zero.
3. Write a program to find the GCD (Greatest Common Divisor) of two numbers using a while and a for loop. For example, Two input numbers are 46 and 9. The GCD of the two numbers is 1.

4. Write a program to find the largest among the three numbers using:
   (a) if and logical and (&&) operator (b) Nested if-else statement
5. Write a program to display the following patterns. In this program user will enter the size of the pattern in terms of the rows, and based on that, the pattern will adjust.

* * * * * * * * * * * * * * *	* * * * * * * * * * * * * * *	* *	* *
1 1 2 1 2 3 1 2 3 4 1 2 3 4 5	1 2 3 4 5 1 2 3 4 1 2 3 1 2 1	1 2 3 2 3 4 5 4 3 4 5 6 7 6 5 4 5 6 7 8 9 8 7 6 5	1 1 1 1 2 1 1 3 3 1 1 4 6 4 1 1 5 10 10 5 1

KNOW MORE

Flowchart. The flowchart is a way to show the proper flow of the process. It is the diagrammatical representation of the process's execution. In the flowchart, the box represents the steps involved in the task's execution, and the arrow represents the order of the step's execution. The flowchart consists of symbols to represent the steps involved in the task's execution. The description of the common symbols is shown below.

Symbol	Name	Description
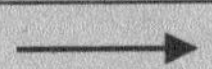	Flowline	Flowline used to connect two symbols. The head of the flowline (arrow) represent the flow of the process.
	Terminal	It is used to show the starting and ending point of the process.
	Process	The rectangle box used to show the process.
	Input/Output	The parallelogram used to represent the input/output steps.
	Decision	The diamond shape used to represent the decision step in the flow chart.

Example: Suppose we want to check whether a given number is even or odd.

For the above example, we have to follow the following steps:

1. Take a number from the user

2. To Check whether the given number is even or odd we will divide it by 2 (In c language the modulus operator used to find the reminder).
   - If we get reminder 0, the number will be even; otherwise, it will be odd.

For the better understanding these steps can be represented by the flowchart

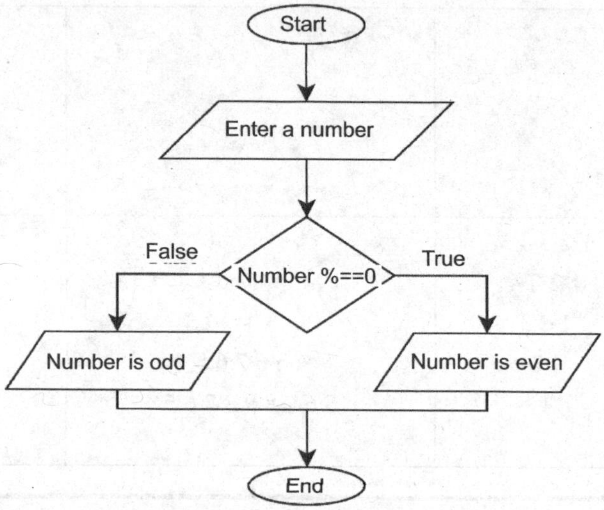

Fig. 3.31: Flowchart to check even or odd number

REFERENCES AND SUGGESTED READINGS

1. Deitel, P. J. (2015). *C how to Program: With an Introduction to C++* ***(Chapter 3 and Chapter4)***. Pearson Education India.
2. David Griffiths and Dawn Griffiths (2011). Head First C, O'Reilly Media, Inc.
3. https://nptel.ac.in/courses/106104128
4. https://nptel.ac.in/courses/106105171 *(lectures for week 3 and week 4)*

Dynamic QR Code for Further Reading

The author has created supporting video lectures for each unit. Readers are encouraged to watch the lectures to better understand the topics covered in Unit III. However, it is advised to read the book units first and then see the videos. The video lectures may not cover the whole unit but are provided as supplementary material.

4 Arrays and Functions in C

UNIT SPECIFICS

Through this unit, we have discussed the following aspects:

- Use of different Arrays and Functions in C
- To learn Array Declaration and Initialization
- To learn Function Declaration in C
- Learn different ways of Function Calling in C
- Advantages of using Functions
- Practice problems on various Arrays and Functions in C

All these topics are discussed with detailed examples. Further, if needed, there is reference material attached to each topic. To maintain the curiosity and interest of the readers, this unit also provides video links via QR code to explain each topic. At the end of the unit, various exercises are provided that include Multiple Choice Questions (MCQs), output-based questions, practical exercises, etc. Moreover, a list of references and suggested readings are given at the end of the unit.

RATIONALE

In this unit, we introduce Array and Function in computer programming. An array is useful when we want to solve computation problems that involve a large set of data. Moreover, functions are used to bring modularity and reusability to the program. Therefore, these two concepts are beneficial in writing computer programs for complex sets of problems. This unit begins with the introduction of Arrays and Functions in C, followed by examples. Next, it discusses the Arrays, Array Declaration, and Initialization of arrays in C, followed by various operations of arrays. Next, it discusses memory organization and introduces the concept of pointers in C. It also discusses the string as character arrays in C. Next, it starts with the Function, its advantages, and different types of functions. It covers the syntax of various functions with demonstrative examples and benefits. A brief introduction to the storage classes is also discussed in this unit.

PRE-REQUISITES

Unit-I, II, and III

UNIT OUTCOMES

List of outcomes of this unit is as follows:

U4-O1: Describe the need for Array and Function in problem-solving using C

U4-O2: Describe the memory organization in C

U4-O3: Explain syntax and usage of Array C programming

U4-O4: Explain the syntax and usage of Function in C programming

U4-O5: Apply Array and function in problem-solving using C

Unit-4 Outcomes	EXPECTED MAPPING WITH COURSE OUTCOMES (1- Weak Correlation; 2- Medium correlation; 3- Strong Correlation)					
	CO-1	CO-2	CO-3	CO-4	CO-5	CO-6
U4-O1	-	3	2	3	-	-
U4-O2	1	3	2	2	-	-
U4-O3	2	2	3	2	-	1
U4-O4	2	2	3	2	-	1
U4-O5	2	2	3	2	-	3

4.1 INTRODUCTION

In the previous Units, we studied the various primitives in C programming, including Data types (int, float, double, and char), types of instructions, and control statements. Throughout the book, we considered data as a single element of one of these data types. In all the practical examples, we take variables for holding input and output data. However, a software/program might work on a large amount of data. Consider the following example.

> ***Example.*** Consider a scenario where you want to develop a program to calculate the average marks in a subject for 200 students in a class. One way is to define 200 variables of int (or double) data type and then carry out 200 scanf() operations to store the inputted values in the variables and then find out the average among these variables.

This can become more complicated when you want to do operations on a large number of elements, let's say 100000. Declaring and handling variables for each data element would be very difficult.

However, if you observe in the given an example, all the 200 values are of the same type and have the same semantics (i.e., all values represent marks), thus it can be represented as a single variable (let's say marks) that can hold 200 elements and **some way to access** individual marks value. That is where an **Array** is helpful in programming. Therefore, in another way, we can store the marks of 200 students in a single integer **array**, apply a loop to store all 200 values entered by a user, and then compute the average.

Which option do you think is better? The second option, which involves storing the same data types in a single variable and later accessing them via an array index, is more practical. (we will discuss it in the following section).

4.2 ARRAY

An array is a group of *contiguous* memory locations that all have the *same type.* We provide the name of the array and the **position number** of the specific element in the array to refer to a specific location or element in the array.

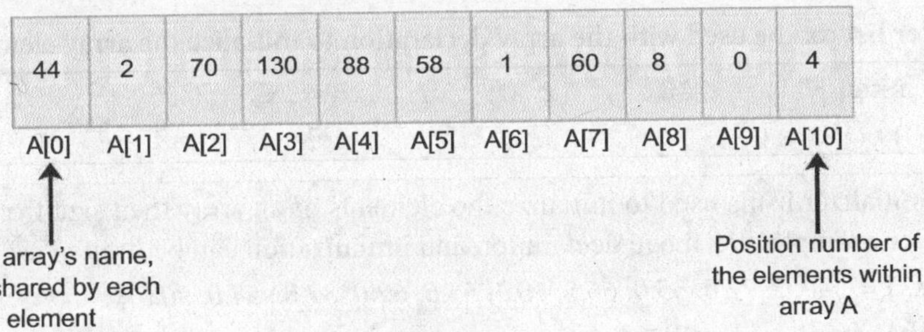

Fig . 4.1: Array Example

Fig. 4.1 depicts an integer array called A, which consists of 11 **elements.** You can refer to any of these elements by putting the array's name followed by the element's position number in square brackets ([ ]). The first element in every array is the **zeroth element** (i.e., the one with position number 0). Similar to other identifiers, an array name cannot start with a digit and can only contain letters, numbers, and underscores.

Question 4.1 Why is the array index starts from 0? Why not 1?

4.2.1 Array Declaration and Initialization

In C language, the array is declared as follows.

```
data_type array_name[size];
```

Similar to any other variable declaration, we specify the type of data (`int, char, float` etc.) and `array_name` (an identifier) and the `size` of the array (an integer constant) that specifies the number of elements in the array. The name of array (i.e., `array_name`) should follow the valid identifier name rule studied in Unit I. For example, `'Marks'` is the variable name of size 10 having a datatype double.

```
double Marks[10];
```

i.e., the given array can hold 10 mark values (may correspond to 10 students). Any individual mark value can be accessed by providing an index number (starting from 0 to 9). We can initialize an array by putting values one by one using an array index (*rarely used*).

```
Marks[0] = 40.5;
Marks[1] = 72.0;
..
..
Marks[10] = 90.5;
```

or an **initializer list** can be used with the array declaration to initialize the array elements. For example,

```
double Marks[10] = {40.5, 72.0, 35.0, 66.5, 10.5, 55.5, 62.0, 87.0,
54.0, 90.5};
```

Note: If an initializer list is used to initialize the elements of an array then size from declaration can be omitted. For example, the above declaration and initialization can be written as:
double Marks[ ] = {40. 5, 72.0, 35.0, 66.5, 10.5, 55.5, 62.0, 87.0, 54.0, 90.5};
In this case, the compiler identifies the size of an array by the size of the initializer list.

Question 4.2: What would happen if we put less number of values in the initializer list than the size of an array (case 1)? Similarly, if we give more values in the initializer list than the size of an array (case 2)?

```
double Marks[10] = {40. 5, 72.0, 35.0, 66.5, 10.5, 55.5,
62.0}; //Case 1

double Marks[10] = {40. 5, 72.0, 35.0, 66.5, 10.5, 55.5,
62.0, 87.0, 54.0, 90.5, 40.5}; //Case 2
```

Scan QR code for Answer

Accessing an element in Array: An index number in between square brackets specifies a location to access a particular element in the array. For example, if you want to access '72.0' (second element), then you can write the statement `Marks[1]` (index starts from 0 therefore, 72.0 is at first position). Similarly, `Marks[9]` will return 90.5.

Note: In C programming, if you try to access elements outside the size of the array, the compiler won't give you an error; instead, you might get a garbage value. Therefore, it is the responsibility of the programmer to check/use index numbers in Array carefully.

Runtime Array Initialization: The above-mentioned initialization can be termed compile-time initialization. Whereas, if we want to initialize the array by taking input from the user, we can use loops. A simple example is shown in Fig.4.2.

```
1. #include<stdio.h>
2. #define SIZE 10
3. int main(){
4.     double marks[SIZE];
5.      for(int var1=0;var1<size; var1++){
6.         scanf("%f", &marks[var1]);
7.      }
8.   return 0;
9. }
```

Fig. 4.2: Runtime initialization of an array

In the above example, line number 2 defines a constant for array size. Line number 4 declares an array 'marks' of type double. A `for` loop (line number 5) is used to demonstrate the initialization of the array.

> **Programming Tip:** It is a good practice to define array size as a macro constant. Whenever a programmer wants to change the size of an array, it has to change at only one place, and it will be reflected throughout the program.

Memory allocation and address representation in an array. In unit I, we briefly discussed memory structure in computers. Computer memory is split into tiny units called bytes. Each byte has a unique address. Array stores in computer in a continuous manner. i.e., all the elements are stored in continuous locations in the memory. For example, if the memory address of the first element of an integer type array is 2000, then the next element will be stored at the location 2004 address (assuming the integer occupies 4 bytes), and so on. An example is shown in Fig 4.3.

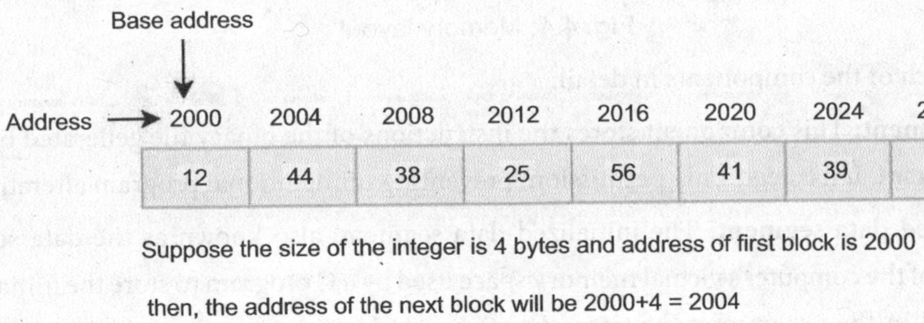

Fig. 4.3: Memory allocation and address representation in an array

Before discussing the further concepts using array and function. It is better to understand the memory layout in the C programming language.

4.3 MEMORY ORGANIZATION IN C

As we already know, a computer program is stored in secondary storage and must be brought into the primage storage (RAM) for its execution. Since RAM storage is limited, the programmer must utilize the limited space efficiently. Knowing the memory layout in C helps programmers to decide the amount of memory to be utilized by their computer program.

The memory layout in C contains five basic components: Text segment, Initialized data segment, uninitialized data segment, Stack, and Heap. Each component stores a different part of the code with its exclusive read and writes permissions. The diagram of the memory layout is shown in Fig. 4.4

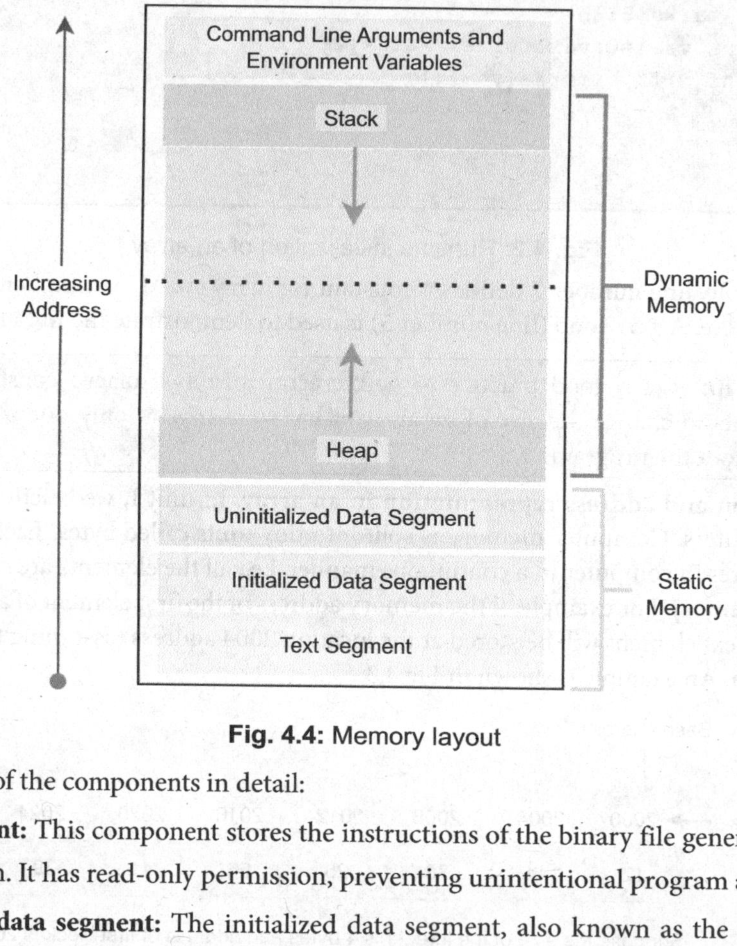

Fig. 4.4: Memory layout

We'll discuss each of the components in detail:

1. **Text segment:** This component stores the instructions of the binary file generated by compiling a C program. It has read-only permission, preventing unintentional program alterations.
2. **Initialized data segment:** The initialized data segment, also known as the data segment, is a portion of the computer's virtual memory space used by a C program to store the initialized values (initiated in the program at the time of variable declaration) for all `external, global, static, and constant` variables that were declared in the program (dicussed in Section 4.8). It has read-write permissions since the value of the variables can be changed during the execution. Also, read-only permission for the constant variables since their value remains the same throughout the execution.
3. **Uninitialized data segment:** This segment stores all the uninitialized `global, local, and external` variables which were not initialized in the program. It initializes the variables to zero and the pointer to null pointer. It is also known as the bss(block started by symbol) segment. It has read-write permission.

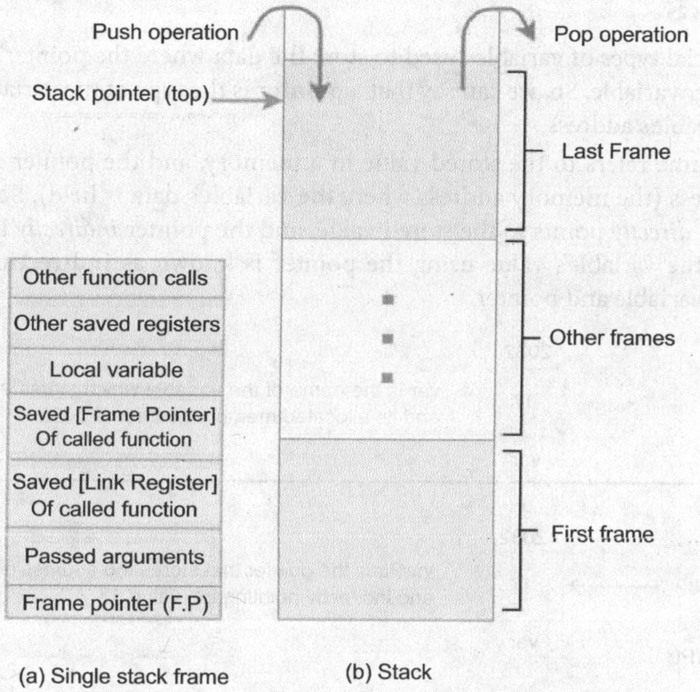

Fig. 4.5: Visualization and components of the stack

4. **Stack:** The stack segment is used for the dynamic memory allocation. It grows and shrinks in the opposite direction of the Heap, as shown in Fig 4.5. The stack segment uses a stack data structure to store the data, which follows the First In last Out (FILO) or Last In First Out (LIFO) properties. The stack has a top pointer that always points to the top of the stack (points to the recently added data). The top (pointer) is used to modify or access the stack's data. In stack, the insertion of the data is known as the push operation, and the deletion of the data is known as the pop operation. Both (push and pop) operations are performed from the top of the stack. In every push operation, the top (pointer) will increase by 1, and then data will be put on the location pointed by the top. In pop operation, first data will remove from the top of the stack, then the top (pointer) will decrease by 1. Stack has one type of container known as the stack frame. The stack uses this stack frame to store the value of the local variables, temporary variables, the parameters passed to a function, and the return address (shown in Fig 4.5 (a)). At the time of the push operation, the stack creates the stack frame and stores the respective data in it. Stack also manages the order of the function call. That means if we have a series of the function calling (function called inside the function), the function called at the last will be executed first (LIFO behavior), shown in Fig 4.5.
5. **Heap:** It is used for allocating the memory during the run time. The functions *malloc(), calloc(),* and *realloc()* is used for allocating the memory in the heap segment. It grows and shrinks in the opposite direction of the Stack.

4.4 POINTERS

Scan for further reading

Pointers are the special types of variables used to store the data where the pointer's data is an address of another variable. So, we can say that a **pointer** is the type of the variable used to store another variable's address.

The variable name refers to the stored value in a memory, and the pointer refers to that memory's address (the memory address where the variable's data is held). So we can say that the variable *directly* points to the stored value, and the pointer *indirectly* indicates the variable's value. Referencing the variable's value using the pointer is known as **indirection**. Fig 4.6 shows the visualization of the variable and pointer.

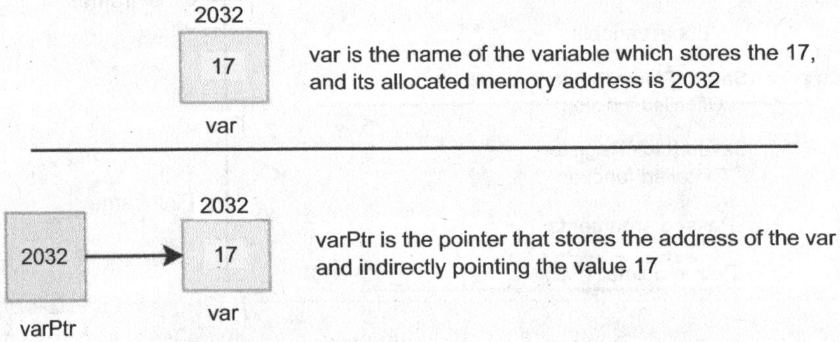

Fig. 4.6: Visualization of the variable and pointer

As we know, the variable should be defined before use. The pointer is also a variable, so in this sense, the pointer must be defined before use.

Syntax to define the pointer

```
data_type *pointer_name;
```

Before using the pointer in C, we must understand the two operators:

1. **ampersand (&) operator:** The ampersand (`&`) operator is used to get the address of the variable. This address is used to access the data (value) of the variable. For example, suppose we have a variable `var` and `varPtr` is a pointer. So, `&var` gives the address of the `var` variable, and it can be stored in the `varPtr` (shown below).

```
varPtr= &var;
```

2. **asterisk (*) operator:** The asterisk operator is used for two purposes.

To declare a pointer: The first use of the asterisk operator is to declare the pointer. During the pointer variable declaration, the asterisk operator is written before the pointer's name (as shown in the syntax to define the pointer).

To access the value of the stored address: The second use of the asterisk operator is to access the value of the stored address. As we know, the pointer is used to store the address of the variable. So the name of the pointer always pointing the address of the variable. To access the variable's value, programmers need to use the asterisk operator, which returns the value of the corresponding address. It is also called **dereferencing**.

```
1.  #include <stdio.h>
2.  int main()
3.  {
4.        int var=21;
5.        int *varPtr;
6.        varPtr=&var;

7.        printf("Value of the variable: %d\n",var);
8.        printf("Address of the variable: %d\n",&var);
9.        printf("Value of the pointer: %d\n",varPtr);
10.       printf("After dereferencing: %d",*varPtr);

11.       return 0;
12. }
13.
```

Fig. 4.7: Demonstration of the pointer

In the above example (Fig 4.7), line 5 `varPtr` pointer is declared using the asterisk. In line 6, the ampersand operator is used to get the address of the `var` and store it in the `varPtr`. Lines 7, 8, 9, and 10 show the results with respect to the variable and the pointer. Here we can see that `varPtr` and `&var` print the same values, and `*varPtr` and `var` print the same values.

Output

```
Value of the variable: 21
Address of the variable: 1723142460
Value of the pointer: 1723142460
After dereferencing: 21
```

4.4.1 Arithmetic Operation in Pointer

As we know that the pointer is used to store the address; that is why minimal arithmetic operations can be performed on pointers. In a pointer, valid arithmetic operations are:

1. **Increment and decrement of a pointer:** The pointer supports the increment and decrement operators. The increment operator sends the pointer to the next address by adding the appropriate value (the data type size) instead of 1. Similarly, the decrement operator sends the pointer to the previous address by subtracting the appropriate value (the data type size) instead of 1. The demonstration is shown in Fig.4.8.
2. **Addition and subtraction of an integer in a pointer:** The addition and subtraction of an integer in a pointer also work like an increment or decrement operation shown in Fig.4.8.

For example, suppose we add 4 to the pointer; that means 4*(`sizeof`(datatype)) will be added to the address, and the pointer will shift to the fourth address from the current. Similarly, if we subtract 4 from the pointer, then the pointer will shift back to the 4th address.

```
#include <stdio.h>
int main()
{
    int var=21;
    int *varPtr;
    varPtr=&var;

    printf("Value of the pointer: %d\n",varPtr);
    printf("After increment: %d\n",++varPtr);
    varPtr=varPtr+2;
    printf("After adding 2: %d\n",varPtr);
    printf("After decrement: %d\n",--varPtr);
    varPtr=varPtr-2;
    printf("After subtracting 2: %d\n",varPtr);

    return 0;
}
```

Fig. 4.8: Demonstration of the arithmetic operations in pointer

Output

```
Value of the pointer: 1934329196
After increment: 1934329200
After adding 2: 1934329208
After decrement: 1934329204
    After subtracting 2: 1934329196
```

3. **Subtraction between two pointers:** Two pointers can be subtracted from each other if their types are similar.
4. **Comparison of the pointers:** Two pointers can be compared if their types are similar.

4.4.2 Types of pointers

In C programming, there are three types of pointers.

Void pointer: A pointer with no data type is known as a void pointer. The void pointer is declared by using the void data type. A void pointer is also known as a general-purpose pointer. This pointer can point to some memory location which means it can point to the address of the variable. In the C programming language, `malloc()` and `calloc()` return the void type address.

For example, `void *varPtr1;`

Null Pointer: This pointer can be created by assigning the Null (zero) value during the declaration of the pointer.

For example, `int *varPtr2= NULL;`

Wild pointer: A pointer with no value is known as a wild pointer. The wild pointer can be dangerous for the program. It can cause the crash of the program. The best practice is to initialize the pointer while declared.

For example, `int *varPtr3;` // without initializing any address or Null value

```
1.  #include <stdio.h>
2.  int main()
3.  {
4.      void *varPtr1;            // Void type pointer
5.      int *varPtr2= NULL;      // Null pointer
6.      int *varPtr3;            // Wild pointer

7.      printf("void type pointer: %d\n",varPtr1);
8.      printf("Null pointer: %d\n",varPtr2);
9.      printf("Wild pointer: %d\n",*varPtr3);

10.     return 0;
11. }
```

Fig. 4.9: Demonstration of different types of pointers

In the above example (Fig. 4.9), void, null and wild pointers are declared in lines 4, 5, and 6, respectively. In the output, we can see that the void pointer has located some memory by default. In line 9, we try to dereference the wild pointer, but it gives the segment fault because it did not point to any memory location.

Output:

```
void type pointer: 328965584
Null pointer: 0
Segmentation fault
```

4.5 STRING AS ARRAY OF CHARACTERS

A string is a sequence of characters ended by a null character '\0'. As we have learned in Unit 1, the C language does not allow String data type. The C language supports String as a 1-D (dimensional) array of characters. Now, we will see how to declare and initialize strings. The basic syntax is as follows.

```
char s_nme[size];
```

where `s_nme` is the string name and `size` represents the string size. For example, the `bird` is the name of the string, which contains at most 10 characters, including a null character.

```
char bird[8];
```

4.5.1 Initialization of a String

There basic syntax of initializing a string at the compile time is as follows:

```
char bird[]= "PEACOCK";
```

This initializes the string variable `bird` to "`Peacock.`" It creates an array of characters of size 8 containing `'P'`, `'E'`, `'A'`, `'C'`, `'O'`, `'C'`, `'K'`, and `'\0'`. The above initialization can also be written as:

```
char bird[]= {'P', 'E', 'A', 'C', 'O', 'C', 'K', '\0'}; \\ null character
is explicitly mentioned
```

Here, the size of a string `bird` can be identified by the compiler depending on the characters present in the initializer's list. We have to explicitly mention the null character '\0' during the initialization. In contrast, the compiler automatically appends a null character to the end when the string is initialized within double quotation marks.

4.5.2 Reading a String from User

When the user initializes the string at run time, the `scanf` function is used to take the input from the user. The syntax is given below.

```
scanf("%s",array_name);
```

Here, the `'%s'` format specifier is used for strings, and `'&'` is not appended with the `array_name` as the array's name represent the base address. The example is given below:

```
scanf("%s", bird);
```

A C program is shown in Fig.4.10 that demonstrates to read a string from the user:

```
#include<stdio.h>

int main()
{
char bird[10]; // declaring a string bird of size 10
printf("Enter the string ");
scanf("%s",bird); //taking input from user
printf("The value of a string is %s", bird); //printing the value of string
return 0;
}
```

Fig. 4.10: Demonstration to read a string from the user

Output (Assuming input is PEACOCK)

```
Enter the string PEACOCK
The value of a string is PEACOCK
```

Question 4.4: What if a user wants to enter the sentence "Peacock is a bird"?

As we all know, `scanf()` reads the input until it encounters whitespaces. Sentences consist of many whitespaces. So, another function `gets()`, is available in the `stdio.h` library is used for reading a sentence as input. It treats whitespaces as a part of a string. Similarly, `puts()` is used to display a sentence.

4.6 MULTIDIMENSIONAL ARRAY

A multidimensional array is a collection of arrays used to hold homogenous. The simplest form of a multidimensional array is a 2-D array. We need to specify two dimensions to recognize a specific element in a table. The first dimension specifies the element's row, and the second represents the element's column (by default). The syntax for declaring the 2-D array is shown below:

```
data_type  arr_name[size_1][size_2];
```

For example,

```
int marks[3][4];
```

`marks` is a 2-D array of type float. The number of elements an array holds is calculated by multiplying all the dimensions of an array. The `marks` array holds 12 elements (3*4). The representation of the marks array is shown in Fig 4.11.

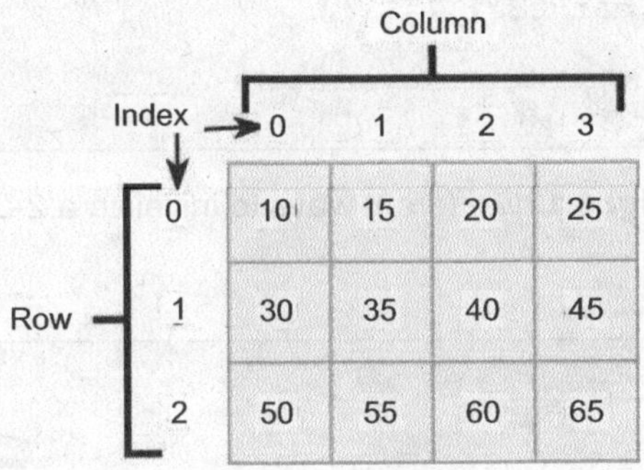

Fig. 4.11: Representation of 2-Dimensional Array (`marks`)

To access an element of a marks array, we need to specify the row number followed by a column number. For example, `marks[2][3]=65, marks[0][1]=15, marks[1][2]=40`

> Note: For creating an n-D array, we must specify n-subscript (dimensions) while declaring an array. For example, `float marks[size_1][size_2]...[size_n];`

An example to demonstrate 2-D array is shown in Fig 4.12.

```
#include<stdio.h>

int main()
{
//compile time initialization of a mark1 and mark2 array
int marks1[2][3]= {10,15,20,25,30,35};
int marks2[2][3] = {{10,15},{20,25},{30,35}};
int marks3[2][3];
printf("The elements of mark1 array are:\n");
for(int i=0;i<2;i++){
   for(int j=0; j<2;j++){
```

```
      printf("%d\n",marks1[i][j]);}
}
printf("The elements of mark2 array are:\n");
for(int i=0;i<2;i++){
  for(int j=0; j<3;j++){
      printf("%d\n",marks2[i][j]);}
}
//run time initialization of mark3 array
for(int i=0;i<2;i++){
  for(int j=0; j<3;j++){
      printf("Enter the values for marks[%d][%d]", i,j);
      scanf("%d",&marks3[i][j]);}
}
for(int i=0;i<3;i++){
  for(int j=0; j<4;j++){
      printf("%d\n",marks3[i][j]);}
}
}
```

Fig. 4.12: Different ways to initialize a 2-D array

Output

```
The elements of marks1 array are:
10
15
20
25
30
35 The elements of marks2 array are:
10
15
0
20
25
0
Enter the values for marks[0][0] 1
Enter the values for marks[0][1] 2
Enter the values for marks[0][2] 3
Enter the values for marks[1][0] 4
Enter the values for marks[1][1] 5
Enter the values for marks[1][2] 6
```

```
The elements of marks3 array are:
1
2
3
4
5
6
```

The tabular representation of an array is for the programmer's simplicity (as shown in Fig. 4.11). However, the arrays are stored in `row-major` or `column-major` order. In `row-major` order, the elements are arranged linearly row-wise, whereas, in `column-major` order, the elements are arranged linearly column-wise. Both representations are shown in Fig. 4.13:

Question 4.5: How multidimensional arrays are stored in memory?

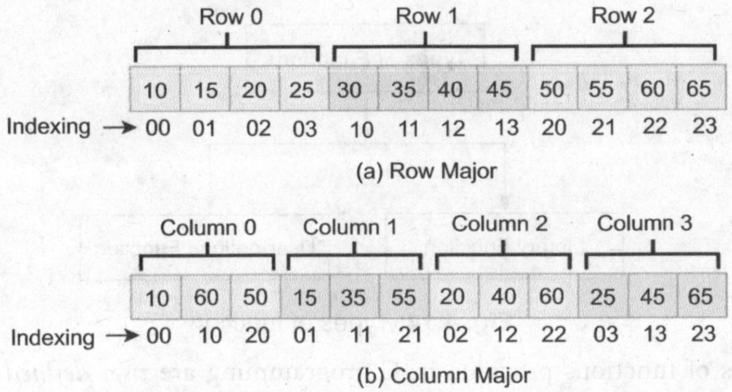

Fig. 4.13: 2-Dimensional array (`marks`) representation in a row and column-major order

4.7 FUNCTION

We, humans, depend on many people, knowingly or unknowingly, for many different things. Despite being intelligent, we cannot complete all life's tasks independently. For example, A person may call a mechanic to repair his car, employ a gardener to prune his lawn, and depend on a grocery store to deliver foodstuff monthly. Similarly, A computer program (other than the simple programs studied in previous chapters) faces an analogous situation; it cannot complete every task by itself. Instead, it requires program-like entities known as functions to complete the task. This section discusses the use of functions in a programming language.

A **function** can be defined as a set of statements that collectively performs some task. It takes inputs, performs the tasks, and returns the results. A function must be declared first before calling in the program. We can call the function several times. As we have already seen, using a function is similar to employing a person to carry out an assigned task. Getting along with the person is sometimes easy and challenging. For example, consider a routine operation you conduct, such as repairing your motorcycle every two months in the same manner as before. When the time comes, you visit the service center and request its service. The individual does not need to provide instructions because the mechanic is experienced in his work. When the task is done, you do not need to be informed. You expect that the mechanic will perform the standard maintenance on the bike, and that will be all. A simple C function works identically as the mechanic. A function is also known as a method, procedure, or routine.

4.7.1 Advantages of using Functions

The advantages of using Functions are as follows:

1. Code reusability (Avoids repetition of codes)
2. Increases program readability
3. Divides large complex problems into simple ones.
4. Reduces the chance of errors.

4.7.2 Types of Functions

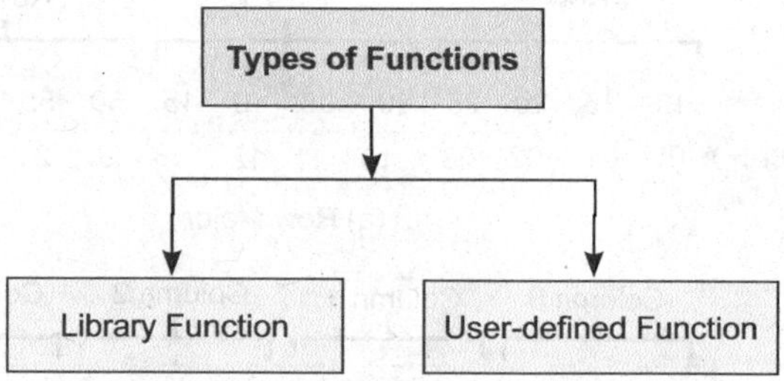

Fig. 4.14: Types of function

The two kinds of functions provided in C programming are *user-defined* and *library functions* (shown in Fig. 4.14). **Library functions** are built-in functions that perform a specific task and are present in standard libraries. The header files are used to include these standard libraries. Programmers are not required to write library functions. A C program uses a variety of built-in functions that are present in the standard C library. For example, `printf()` and `scanf()` are defined in the `stdio.h` library, while `cbrt()` for computing the cube of a number and `pow()` for the computing power of a number is defined in `math.h` library. **User-defined functions** are required to be written by the programmer while creating the code. These functions need to be declared and defined by the programmer itself.

4.7.3 Function Definition, Declaration, and Calling

Now, we will learn how to write custom (user-defined) functions. Before writing a custom function, we must know the answers to three questions. 1. How to define a function? 2. How is a function declared? 3. How is a function called? We will start with the function definition.

Defining a function: The function definition defines the actual body of the function. A function comprises a header and body. The first line of the function definition is called the function header, which comprises three parts: return data type, function name, and argument list. The syntax is shown below.

```
return_data_type fun_name(arg_list) //function header
{
   set of statements; // function body
}
```

- **return_data_type** - It defines the data types of value that a function returns after executing its function body. The default return type is int. It is not necessary for a function to always return a value. Sometimes, it returns nothing; in such cases, the void return type is used.
- **fun_name** - It specifies the function name. It should be a valid identifier.
- **arg_list** - It is a list of arguments separated by commas received when the function is called. When a function is called, the value to the arguments is passed. The argument list is void if no value is passed through the function.
- **function_body** - It comprises a set of statements that describe the function's functionality.

The control can be passed to the called function in various ways (back to the place from where the function was called). When the function returns nothing, the control is transferred when the right curly brace of the function is encountered, or it can be accomplished by executing the following statement.

```
return;
```

When the function returns a value, the statement

```
return expression;
```

is used to return the value to the point from which it has been invoked. Here, an expression could be a value or an expression. For example, a function finds the smallest number among two and returns the smallest number.

```
int smallest(int var1 , int var2) //function definition
{
  int small;
  if(var1 > var2)
    small = var2;
  else
    small = var1;
  return small;
}
```

Here, in the above example, a function smallest is defined, which finds the smallest number among the two numbers. This function takes two arguments of integer type and returns an integer value after executing the function's body. The variable declared inside the function's body, that is, small is the local variable. It is identified within the function smallest in which it is defined.

Function Declaration: It is also known as a function prototype. It informs the compiler of the type of data the function returns, the number and types of arguments the function receives, and the order in which the arguments appear. The compiler ensures the correctness of the function call by checking the function prototype. The syntax is as follows:

```
return_data_type function_name(argument_list);
```

For example, the function declaration of the `smallest` function is shown below.

```
int smallest (int, int);    // function prototype
```

The function declaration of the smallest function states that this function takes two integer-type arguments as an input and returns an integer value as an output. We can also give variable names in the argument list shown in Fig 4.15. It should be noted that the first line of the function definition and declaration is the same. A compilation error occurs when they both differ.

> **Note:** The function declaration results in a syntax error if the semicolon is left off at the end of the function declaration.

Function Calling: We have already seen how to declare and define a function. How can we use the defined function in our C program to perform a specific task? To use it, we need to call the function in the program. The program's control is transferred to the function when a function is called. It performs the task defined in the function's body. After performing the task, it returns the results to the caller function from where it has been called. The syntax is as follows:

```
func_name(argumnent_lst);
```

We need to write the function's name along with the list of arguments. If it returns a value, then a variable should be there to store it. For example,

```
small_number = smallest(a,b); //function call
// small_number stores the result returned by the smallest function.
```

Here, the function named `smallest` is called, which takes three integer arguments as input and returns the integer argument, which will be stored in the variable `small_number`.

The complete program demonstrates the functionality of a function shown in Fig 4.15.

```
#include <stdio.h>
int smallest(int , int);   //function prototype
int main() {
    int a,b,small_number;
    printf("Enter two integer values:");
    scanf("%d %d", &a, &b);

   small_number = smallest(a,b);      //function call
   printf("The smallest number is %d",small_number);

return 0;
}

int smallest(int var1 , int var2) //function definition
{
int small;
if(var1 > var2)
   small = var2;
```

```
else
    small = var1;
return small;
}
```

Fig. 4.15: Demonstration of working of a `smallest` function

Output:

```
Enter two integer values:
23
34
The smallest number is 23
```

***Note:** It is assumed that the user enters 23, and 34 as an input

Consider another example that prints cubes of a number from 1 to 5 using a function cube shown in Fig.4.16.

```
#include <stdio.h>
int cube(int var2);    //function prototype

int main() {
    int var1;
    for(var1=1; var1<=5;var1++)
    {
        printf("%d", cube(var1));    //function call
        printf("\n");
    }
return 0;
}

int cube(int var2)    //function definition
{
return var2 * var2 * var2;
}
```

Fig. 4.16: Demonstration of working of a `cube` function

Output:

```
1
8
27
64
125
```

4.7.4 Function Calling

C programming provides two ways: call by value and call by reference of function calling. Before going into details, we must know the **actual** and **formal** arguments. The arguments which are passed during the function calling are known as actual arguments. The calling function defines these arguments. The actual arguments do not need to have the data type specified. For example,

```
small_number = smallest(a,b); // Here, a & b are the actual arguments.
```

The arguments that are used in the argument_list of the function definition are known as formal arguments. They are defined in the function definition. The data type must be specified in the formal arguments.

```
int smallest (int var1, int var2) //var1 and var2 are the formal arguments
{
    // body of the smallest function
}
```

Call by value: The actual arguments value gets copied into the formal ones in case of call by value. First, copy of actual argument is made, and then it gets passed to the formal arguments in the called function. If the function made any changes to the formal arguments (copied one), it does not reflect the changes back to the actual arguments (present in the caller function). It is used when the invoked function does not intend to alter the value of the caller function. The example is shown in Fig 4.17.

```
#include<stdio.h>
void swap(int, int);
void main( ){
   int var1,var2;
   printf("Enter the two numbers \n");
   scanf("%d", &var1);
   scanf("%d", &var2);
   printf("\nThe values of var1 and var2 before swapping are var1=%d var2=%d",var1,var2);
   swap(var1,var2);
   printf("\n The values of var1 and var2 after swapping (in main function) are var1=%d var2=%d",var1,var2);
  return 0;
}

void swap(int var1, int var2)
{
    int t;
    t= var1;
    var1=var2;
    var2=t;
      printf("\n The values of var1 and var2 after swapping are var1=%d var2=%d",var1,var2);
}
```

Fig. 4.17: Demonstration of call by value method of function calling

Output:

```
Enter the two numbers
34
45
The values of var1 and var2 before swapping are var1=34 var2=45
The values of var1 and var2 after swapping are var1=45 var2=34
The values of var1 and var2 after swapping (in main function) are
var1=34 var2=45
```

***Note:** It is assumed that the user enters 34, 45 as an input

In the above example, we created a swap function to swap two integer numbers using the call-by-value. The function is called from the main function. The actual arguments were copied and passed to the formal arguments. The changes were made in the formal arguments, not the actual ones. We can see that the values were swapped inside the function. However, the changes (swapped values) were not reflected in the main function. The values inside the main function before and after swapping are the same.

Call by Reference

In this, the actual arguments' address is passed to the formal arguments. The address of the actual argument is copied and passed to the formal arguments. The function performs the task with the help of the formal arguments only since the actual and formal arguments both point to the same memory locations. Therefore, any changes performed during a function call will be reflected in the actual arguments of the called function. The call-by-reference method can manipulate the actual arguments (original value). The example is shown in Fig. 4.18.

```
#include<stdio.h>
void swap(int *, int *);
void main( ){
     int var1,var2;
     printf("Enter the two numbers \n");
     scanf("%d",&var1);
     scanf("%d",&var2);
      printf("\nThe values of var1 and var2 before swapping are var1=%d
var2=%d",var1,var2);
     swap(&var1,&var2);
      printf("\n The values of var1 and var2 after swapping (in main
function) are var1=%d var2=%d",var1,var2);
    return 0;
}

void swap(int *var1, int *var2)
{
     int t;
     t= *var1;
     *var1= *var2;
```

```
    *var2= t;
      printf("\nThe values of var1 and var2 after swapping are var1=%d
  var2=%d",*var1,*var2);
}
```

Fig. 4.18: Demonstration of call by reference method of function calling

Output:

```
Enter the two numbers
34
45
The values of var1 and var2 before swapping are var1=34 var2=45
The values of var1 and var2 after swapping are var1=45 var2=34
The values of var1 and var2 after swapping (in main function) are
var1=45 var2=34
```

***Note:** It is assumed that the user enters 34, 45 as an input

In the above example, we created a swap function to swap two integer numbers using the call-by-reference. The actual arguments address was copied and carried to the formal arguments. The actual and formal argument both points to a similar memory location. When the function performs the task of swapping, the changes are directly made to the actual arguments.

Another example of function: Here, we will see one example of calculating the length of the hypotenuse of a right-angled triangle by creating a function `hypotenuse_cal` which, takes the two sides of a triangle as input and returns the length of the hypotenuse as output. The two arguments (two sides) and the hypotenuse length should be double-type. The program performs the calculation for three right-angled triangles. The program is shown in Fig. 4.19.

```
#include <stdio.h>
#include <math.h>
double hypotenuse_cal (double side1 , double side2);
int main() {
    double side1, side2;
    for(int count = 1; count <=3 ; count++)
    {
      printf("Enter the two sides \n");
      scanf("%lf", &side1);
      scanf("%lf", &side2);
      printf("The hypotenuse is %lf",hypotenuse_cal(side1 , side2));
      printf("\n");
    }
return 0;
}

double hypotenuse_cal (double side1 , double side2)
{
```

```
    double hypotenuse = sqrt(side1 * side1 + side2 * side2);
    return hypotenuse;
}
```

Fig. 4.19: Program to calculate the length of the hypotenuse of a right-angled triangle

Output:

```
Enter the two sides
23.2
34.44
The hypotenuse is 41.525337
Enter the two sides
45.56
78.6
The hypotenuse is 90.849731
Enter the two sides
87.6
89.5
The hypotenuse is 125.235818
```

***Note:** It is assumed that the user enters 23.2, 34.44, 45.56, 78.6, 87.6, 89.5 as an input

Question 4.6: Can we define the function without declaring it?

If the function is already defined before it is called, then it is not necessary to provide the declaration. The function should be defined before the function call. If the programmer tries to use the function before declaring it, it will result in a compile-time error.

An example is shown in Fig. 4.20 shows that the function can be defined without declaring it.

```
#include <stdio.h>
#include <math.h>
double hypotenuse_cal (double side1 , double side2)
{
  double hypotenuse = sqrt(side1 * side1 + side2 * side2);
  return hypotenuse;
}
int main() {
    double side1, side2;
    for(int count = 1; count <=3 ; count++)
    {
      printf("Enter the two sides \n");
      scanf("%lf", &side1);
      scanf("%lf", &side2);
      printf("The hypotenuse is %lf",hypotenuse_cal(side1 , side2));
      printf("\n");
```

```
    }
  return 0;
}
```

Fig. 4.20: Program to calculate the length of the hypotenuse of a right-angled triangle

4.7.5 Passing Array to Functions

This section will show how arrays can be passed through functions. Sometimes, passing more than one variable of the same type is required for a function. For instance, suppose a function that arranges the ten numbers in ascending order. This function requires passing ten actual parameters through the function call. This would be cumbersome to pass ten different variables through a function. A different approach is to define an array and pass it through the function. Passing an array resolves the complexity; now, the function can be used for any number of variables.

As we already know, the name of an array represents the base address. We only need to pass the array name to the function. The syntax is given below.

```
function_name(array_name);
```

Here, array_name is the name of the array and function_name is the name of the function. For example,

```
cal_average(arr);
```

Now, we must know how to define a function that receives an array as an argument. There are three ways to define a function that receives an array as an argument. The syntax of all three ways is given below.

1. We can see the use of subscript notation [] in the function definition. It tells the compiler that a one-dimensional array is passed through the function. For example,

```
return_type function_name(data_type array_name[]){
...
}
```

For example,

```
float cal_average(float arr[]){
...
}
```

2. The second way is to define the size of the array in the subscript notation []. The syntax is as follows.

```
return_type function_name(data_type array_name[size]){
...
}
```

For example,

```
float cal_average(float arr[10]){
...
}
```

3. The third way is to use the pointer variable to receive the address of an array.

```
return_type function_name(data_type *arrayname){
...
}
```

For example,

```
float cal_average(float *arr)
```

An example is shown in Fig. 4.21. A function `cal_average()` is declared and defined, which computes the average of all the numbers of an array. This function takes an array as an argument and returns the average value.

```
#include <stdio.h>
float cal_average(float arr[]);       //function prototype

int main() {
    float r, arr[]={22.4,45,67,34,89.21};
  r = cal_average(arr) ;              //function call
  printf("The average is %f",r);
  return 0;
}

float cal_average(float arr[])       //function definition
{
    int var1;
    float res, s=0.0;
    for(var1=0;var1<5;++var1)
   {
        s+=arr[var1];
    }
    res =(s/5);
    return res;
}
```

Fig. 4.21: Demonstration of passing an array to functions

Output

```
The average is 51.521996
```

Advantages of using Functions

1. There are many advantages of using functions in a computer program.

2. Code reusability (Avoids repetition of codes)
3. Increases program readability
4. Divides large complex problems into simple ones.
5. Reduces the chance of errors.

4.8 STORAGE CLASSES

Storage classes are used to define the scope of the variables and functions. In the C program, the storage classes control the life of the variables/ functions in the memory and visibilities. The syntax is given below.

```
storage_class var_data_type var_name;
```

In the C programming language has four storage classes:

- auto
- extern
- static
- register

auto: Any variable defined inside the function or block is declared by default as an auto-storage class. It can also be defined using the `auto` keyword. In this storage class, variables can be visible or accessible only within the function or block. The auto variable cannot be accessed outside the function or the block. The auto-storage variable can be accessed inside the nested block (if the variable is defined inside the outer block, it can be accessed inside the inner block, not vice versa).

The auto variables are stored inside the stack memory, and the life of the variables ends outside the block. The default value of the auto storage variable is garbage.

```
1.  #include<stdio.h>
2.  void functionTo_auto()
3.  {
4.      auto int var1 = 32;     // Explicitly declared auto variable
5.      int var2;               //by default declared as auto variable
6.      printf("The value of var1: %d and var2: %d\n",var1,var2);
7.  }
8.
9.  int main()
10. {
11.     printf("Auto Storage Class demonstrated\n");
12.     functionTo_auto();
13.
14.     return 0;
15. }
```

Fig. 4.22: Demonstration of use of the auto variable

In the above example (Fig.4.22), `var1` and `var2` are defined as auto variables in lines 4 and 5, respectively. In line 4, `var1` is defined using the auto keyword, and in line 5, `var2` define as an auto variable by default. As we know, the visibility of the auto variables has within the block, so they cannot be accessed outside the `functionTo_auto` function.

Output

```
Auto Storage Class demonstrated
The value of var1: 32 and var2: 32765
```

extern: External variables are defined using the extern keyword. It is also a global variable that can be used or modified inside the whole program, and the extern variable's life ends after the complete program's execution.

The external variable can be declared multiple times but can be defined only once. We can declare a function as an extern, but as we know, the functions are already accessible from the whole program, so if we declare them as an extern, then it increases the redundancy only.

```
1.  #include <stdio.h>
2.  extern int var1 = 21;          // extern variable (scope: throughout the function)
3.  int var2 = 12;
4.  int main()
5.  {
6.      auto int var3 = 28;        // auto variable (scope: within the function)
7.      extern int var2;           // extern variable (scope: throughout the function)
8.      printf("The auto variable var3 : %d\n", var3);
9.      printf("The extern variables var1 and var2 : %d,%d\n",var1,var2);
10.     var1 = 25;
11.     printf("The updated extern variable var1 : %d\n",var1);
12.     return 0;
13. }
```

Fig. 4.23: Demonstration of the use of extern variable

In the above example (Fig 4.23), `var1` and `var2` are the external variables that are accessible from anywhere during the program's execution. These variables are declared in lines 2 and 7, respectively.

Output

```
The auto variable var3 : 28
The extern variables var1 and var2 : 21,12
The updated extern variable var1 : 25
```

static: The static storage class is used to declare a static variable. The variable is declared static using the static keyword. A static variable preserves the information throughout the program's execution, even if it is out of scope. So the static variable stored the value which is used last in the scope. The static variables are initialized only once and exist till the program execution is completed.

The static variable is stored in the data segment memory and, by default, initialized by 0.

```
1.  #include <stdio.h>
2.  int main()
3.  {
4.     printf("%d",countFunc());
5.     printf("\n%d",countFunc());
6.
7.     return 0;
8.  }
9.  int countFunc()
10. {
11.      static int varcount=0;
12.      varcount++;
13.      return varcount;
14. }
```

Fig. 4.24: Demonstration of the use of static variable

In the above example (Fig 4.24), in the `countFunc` function `varcount` variable is declared static (in line 12). Here we called the `countFunc` function in lines 4 and 5, respectively. In every call, the function will execute freshly, and the value of the `varcount` variable should be `0` (reset), but this has not happened. Because as we know, `varcount` is a `static` function, so it will get memory only once, and re-initialization will not be done. So, the value updated in the previous function call will carry forward for the subsequent function call, and we will get output 1 2 instead of the 1 1.

Output

```
1
2
```

register The storage class register has properties similar to an auto variable. There is only one difference: if the register is available, then the variable declared using the register keyword uses the register for storage. The benefit of this is that the program's execution will be fast. So due to this property, the most frequently used variable is declared as a register variable so that the program's execution will be quick. If the register is unavailable, then the variable only gets the memory.

```
1.  #include <stdio.h>
2.  int main()
3.  {
4.     register char var1 = 'H';
5.     register int var2 = 22;
6.     auto int var3 = 6;
7.     printf("The register variable var1 : %c\n",var1);
8.     printf("The sum of auto and register variable : %d",(var1+var2));
9.     return 0;
10. }
```

Fig. 4.25: Demonstration of use of the register variable

In the above example (Fig 4.25), `var1` and `var2` are declared as register variables in lines 4 and 5, respectively.

Output

```
The register variable var1: H
The sum of auto and register variable: 94
```

UNIT SUMMARY

Introduction

- Array in C is a type of data structure that holds elements of the identical data type
- Array: An array is a group of contiguous memory locations that all have the same type.
    - Accessing an element in Array. A particular element in the array can be accessed by using an index number in between square brackets.
    - Run time Array Initialization, Using runtime initialization user can enter values throughout different runs of program.

Memory Organization in C

- Computer memory is split into tiny units called bytes. Each byte has a unique address.
- Storage classes are used to define the scope of the variables and functions.
    - Text segment: This component stores the instructions of the binary file generated by compiling a C program. It has read-only permission, preventing unintentional program alterations.
    - Initialized data segment: The initialized data segment, also known as the data segment.
    - Uninitialized data segment: This segment stores all the uninitialized global, local, and external variables which were not initialized in the program.
    - Stack: The stack segment is used for the dynamic memory allocation.
    - Heap: It is used for allocating the memory during the run time.

Pointers

- The pointer is the most powerful feature of the C language. Pointer provides the luxury to create or modify the dynamic data structure, i.e., stack, queue, linked list, and trees.
    - ampersand (&) operator: The ampersand (&) operator is used to get the address of the variable.
    - asterisk (*) operator: The asterisk operator is used for two purposes, to declare a pointer and access the value of the stored address
    - Subtraction between two pointers: Two pointers can be subtracted from each other if their types are similar.
    - Comparison of the pointers: Two pointers can be compared if their types are similar.

String as Array of characters

- String in C are defined as array of characters.
- String can be initialized in two ways: 1) char Str[10] = "hello"; or char Str[10] = {'h', 'e', 'l', 'l', o, '\0'}. In second way, an extra special character (null character) needs to be specified explicitly.
- There is specific library call string.h provides various functions to manipulate the strings.

Multidimensional Array

- A multi-dimensional array is a collection of arrays used to hold homogenous data in tabular form (rows and columns).

Functions

- A function can be defined as a set of statements that collectively performs some task. It takes inputs, performs the tasks, and outputs the results.
    - It provides Code reusability (Avoids repetition of codes)
    - Increases program readability
    - It divides significant complex problems into simple ones.
    - It reduces the chance of errors.
- Defining a function. The function definition provides the actual body of the function. A function consists of a function header and a function body.
    - return_type, It specifies the data types of value that a function returns after executing its function body.
    - function_name, It specifies the name of the function. It should be a valid identifier.
    - argument_list, It is a comma-separated list of arguments. It specifies the arguments received by a function when it is invoked.
    - function_body, the function's body consists of a set of statements that defines the functionality of the function.
- Function Calling. When a program calls a function, the program's control is transferred to the called function. The called function performs the task defined in its body.
    - Call by value. When function called then the value of the actual arguments gets copied into the formal arguments. First, the copy of the actual argument is made, and then it gets passed to the formal arguments in the called function.
    - Call by Reference. In this case, the actual arguments' address is passed to the formal arguments. The address of the actual argument is copied and passed to the formal arguments.

Storage classes

- Storage classes are used to define the scope of the variables and functions. In the C program, the storage classes control the life of the variables/ functions in the memory and visibilities.
    - auto: Any variable defined inside the function or block is declared by default as an auto-storage class.

- extern: External variables are defined using the extern keyword. It is also a global variable that can be used or modified inside the whole program.
- static: The static storage class is used to declare a static variable.
- register: The storage class register has properties similar to an auto variable.

EXERCISES

Multiple Choice Questions

1. If the function return type is not mentioned in the function definition then what would be the default one?
   (a) int
   (b) float
   (c) double
   (d) void
2. Which is not a valid statement (ar1, ar2, and ar3 are integer arrays)?
   (a) ar1 = ar2;
   (b) ar[] = {5,6,3,7};
   (c) ar[5] = {5,8.3,5,2};
   (d) All of the above
3. Which is the correct way to initialize an array in C programming language?
   (a) int ar() = {6,5,4,3,2,1};
   (b) int ar[6] = {6,5,4,3,2,1};
   (c) int ar{6} = {6,5,4,3,2,1};
   (d) int ar{} = {6,5,4,3,2,1};
4. An index of an array starts with
   (a) 0
   (b) 1
   (c) Depends on compiler
   (d) None of the above
5. The output of the code snippet is:

```
int main(){
int ar[8] ={5,6,7,8,9};
printf("%d", ar[5]);
return 0;
}
```

   (a) 9
   (b) 0
   (c) Garbage value
   (d) None of these

ANSWERS									
1.	(a)	2.	(a)	3.	(b)	4.	(a)	5.	(b)

Output-based Questions

What would be the output of the following programs? (Assume stdio.h library is included in each program)

A

```
void compute(int , int);
int main(){
 char var1 =6, var2 = 'A';
 compute(var1, var2);
 return 0;
 }
void compute(int var1, int var2)
{
   printf("%d %d",var1, var2);
}
```

B

```
int main(){
int var1;
for (var1=0;var1<3;var1++)
{
 int var1 =11;
 printf("%d", var1);
 var1++;
}
return 0; }
```

C

```
int main(){
int v;
char c[] = "Computer Programming";
for( v = 0; c[v]!='\0';++v ) {
  if((v%2)==0)
  printf("%c",c[i]); }
return 0;
}
```

D

```
int main() {
 int var1;
 int bg[5] = {1,2,3,4,5};
 bg[1] = ++bg[1];
 var1 =bg[1]++;
 bg[1] = bg[var1++];
 printf("%d,%d", var1,bg[1]);
               return 0;
}
```

E

```
int main() {
                   int bg[] =
 {1,2,3,4,5,6};
 int var1, var2,var3;
 var2 = ++bg[2];
             var3 = bg[1]++;
 var1 = bg[var2++];  printf("va
 r1=%d,var2=%d,var3=%d",var1,v
 ar2,var3);
return 0; }
```

F

```
int main() {
int var1, ar[4] = {4,5,6,7}, r;
r = ar[0];
for(var1=1;var1<4;var1++){
    if(r>ar[var1])
    continue;
    r = ar[var1];  }
 printf("%d",r);
 return 0; }
```

G	H

<pre>int main() {
        int *p, a=100;
p = &100;
printf("%d",*p);
return 0;
}</pre>
	<pre>int main() {
	        int var1 = bg(11);
	printf("%d",--var1);
	return 0; }
	int bg(int var1){
	    return (var1++);
	}</pre>

Answers of Output-based Questions	
A. 6, 65	B. 11 11 11
C. Cmue Pormig	D. 4,4
E. var1=5, var2=5,var3=2	F. 7
G. Compilation Error	H. 10

Short and Long Answer Type Questions

1. Fill in the blanks
   (a) When an array is declared using three subscripts is known as __________ array.
   (b) Can an array store different types of values? (True/Flase)
   (c) An array's ________ is the number used to refer to a specific element.
   (d) When a function returns nothing then, _______ keyword is used.
   (e) The _______ statement passes the value of an expression from where it has been invoked.

Answers

(a) Three-Dimensional (b) False (c) index (d) void
(e) return

2. Write statements to perform the tasks given below:
   (a) Print the sixth element of the character array 'c'.
   (b) Initialize the 5 elements of an integer array 'g' to 1.
   (c) Adding 2 to each of the values of a 'g' array.

Answers

(a) printf("The sixth element is %c", c[5]);
(b) int g[5] ={1,1,1,1,1}; or int g[ ] = {1,1,1,1,1};
(c)
```
for(int i=0; i<5;i++)
{
    g[i] = g[i] +2;
}
```

3. Write a statement to perform the tasks given below: (Variables var1 and var2 are of float types and var1 is initialized to 12.6.
   (a) Declaring a pointer fp of float type.
   (b) Assigning the address of var1 to fp.
   (c) Printing the value pointed by the pointer fp.
   (d) Assigning the address of the var2 to the fp pointer.
   (e) Printing the value pointed by the pointer fp.
   (f) Printing the address stored in the pointer variable.

Answers

```
(a) Float *fp;
(b) fp =&var1
(c) printf("The value pointed by the Pointer fp is %f", *fp );
(d) fp = &var2
(e) printf("The value pointed by the Pointer fp is %f", *fp );
(f) printf("The address stored in the pointer variable is %p", fp);
```

4. Write the function declaration:
   (a) Function `greatest` takes three integer arguments and returns an integer argument.
   (b) Function `intToDouble` takes one integer argument and returns a double (high-precision) number.
   (c) Function `display` takes one integer and one floating-point value and returns nothing. (This function is used for displaying the information)

PRACTICAL

1. Write a C program using functions to perform the following tasks:
   (a) To convert the binary equivalent of a decimal number
   (b) To find the power of a number.
   (c) To reverse the string inputted by the user.
2. Write a program using functions to show a given number as the sum of two prime numbers. For example, 16 can be shown as 16 = 5 +11 and 16 = 3 +13.
3. Write a program to perform the following task:
   (a) Addition of two square matrices
   (b) Subtraction of two square matrices
   (c) Multiplication of two square matrices
   (d) Determinant of a square matrix.
   (e) Inverse of a square matrice (if determinant is non zero)
4. Write a program to take an array of 20 integers as input from the user and create three functions for calculating mean, median, and mode.

KNOW MORE

String Manipulation Functions

C programming language provides a large number of functions for managing strings. These functions are defined in the standard header file `string.h`. These functions are useful for manipulating strings. Some of these functions are given below.

`strcpy(str1,str2)`	It copies a string `str2` into string `str1` and returns the resultant string in `str1`.
`strcat(str1,str2)`	It concatenates a string `str1` to string `str2` and stores the result in the string `str1`. The size of the `str1` should be large enough to store the resultant string; otherwise, it would result in a segmentation fault.
`strlen(str1)`	It computes the length of the string `str1`. This function does not include the null character '\0' while computing the length.
`strcmp(str1,str2)`	It compares the two strings. This function returns zero: if the two strings `str1` and `str2` are equal; positive integer: if the first non-matching character in the `str1` is having a greater ASCII value than that of `str2`. negative integer: if the first non-matching character in the `str1` is having a lower ASCII value than that of `str2`.
`strrev(str1)`	It reverse the string `str1`.
`strlwr(str1)`	It changes the string `str1` to lower case.
`strupr(str1)`	It changes the string `str1` to upper case.

REFERENCES AND SUGGESTED READINGS

1. Deitel, P. J. (2015). *C how to Program: With an Introduction to C++* (***Chapter 5, 6 and 7***). Pearson Education India.
2. David Griffiths and Dawn Griffiths (2011). Head First C, O'Reilly Media, Inc
3. https://nptel.ac.in/courses/106104128
4. https://archive.nptel.ac.in/courses/106/105/106105171/ *(week 6, 7 and 8)*

Dynamic QR Code for Further Reading

The author has created supporting video lectures for each unit. Readers are encouraged to watch the lectures to better understand the topics covered in Unit IV. However, it is advised to read the book units first and then see the videos. The video lectures may not cover the whole unit but are provided as supplementary material.

5 Recursion and Recursive Solutions

UNIT SPECIFICS

Through this unit we have discussed the following aspects:

- Introductions to recursions
- Representation of recursions in C programming
- Types of recursions
- Working on the recursive function
- Recursive Solutions
- Various examples of different recursions
- Practice problems on recursions

All these topics are discussed with detailed examples. Further, if needed, there is reference material attached to each topic. To maintain the curiosity and interest of the readers, this unit also provides video links via QR code to explain each topic. At the end of the unit, various exercises are provided that include Multiple Choice Questions (MCQs), output-based questions, practical exercises, etc. Moreover, a list of references and suggested readings are given at the end of the unit.

RATIONALE

In this unit, we extend the discussion of function introduced in Unit IV. It begins with introducing recursion in C programming, followed by an example. The representations of the base and recursive case are explained. Next, we discuss the type of recursion, direct recursion and indirect recursion. We also discuss different types of direct and indirect recursion with examples. Next, we discuss the possible solutions of recursion with demonstrative C programs. This unit has not only a brief introduction to recursion but also provides direction to the effective use of recursion in various types of problems. The given examples offer insights into the solution to different real-world computation problems. In summary, this unit introduces a new approach to solve complex problems efficiently.

PRE-REQUISITES

Basic Mathematics, Unit-I, II, III and IV

UNIT OUTCOMES

List of outcomes of this unit is as follows:

U5-O1: Describe the need for recursive function in problem-solving using C

U5-O2: Describe types of recursive functions

U5-O3: Explain the uses of recursion through example.

U5-O4: Apply recursive function in problem-solving using C

Unit-5 Outcomes	EXPECTED MAPPING WITH COURSE OUTCOMES (1- Weak Correlation; 2- Medium correlation; 3- Strong Correlation)					
	CO-1	CO-2	CO-3	CO-4	CO-5	CO-6
U5-O1	-	3	2	3	-	-
U5-O2	1	3	2	2	-	-
U5-O3	2	2	3	2	-	1
U5-O4	2	2	3	2	-	3

5.1 INTRODUCTION

When a function calls itself (directly or indirectly) then it is known as the **recursion** in computer programming. Recursion is a technique that breaks complex problems into small sub problems. The dividing of the problem depends upon the base condition. The base condition is the scenario where we stop dividing the problems and return the results. So, in a recursive call problem, it is divided into sub problems until the base condition will not meet.

Example: Suppose you are ready to go office and look for the car key in a key stand in the morning, but you don't find it. At the same time, your child comes out and says I hid the car key in a box. You are getting late and want a car key.

You immediately open the box, but you find one more box inside the box. The child says, the box has a box, and he does not know which box has a key. So now you have to develop an excellent algorithm to find the key.

There are two ways to create an algorithm for the above problem: iterative and recursive. Let us see both ways using the flow chart.

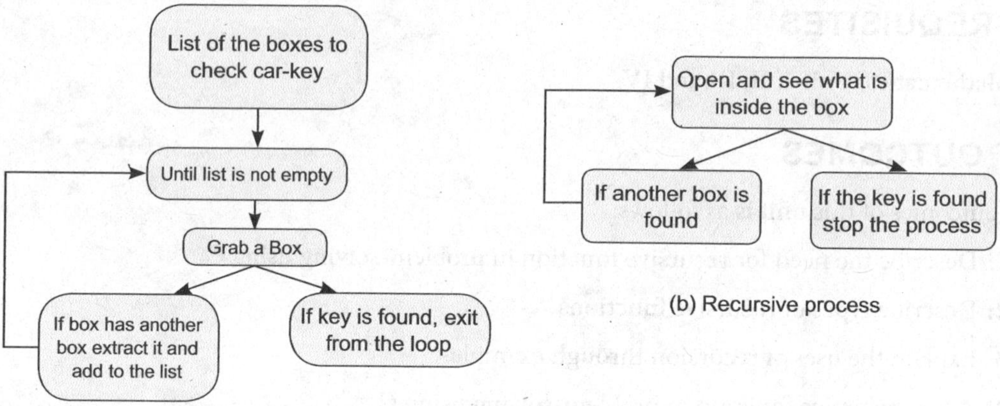

(b) Recursive process

(a) Iterative process

Fig. 5.1: Iterative and Recursive way to find the car key

The first approach (Fig 5.1 (a)) uses a while loop to solve the problem. Here loop checks the box in each iteration; if it has another box; it extracts and adds it to the list. The working of the while loop is already discussed in section 3.4.1.

The second approach (Fig 5.1 (b)) uses a recursive function where it opens the box, and if it has another box, it opens it again. This process will continue until the key fond.

Both approaches did the same thing but in the second approach, we can visualize the solution more easily. There are no performance benefits by using recursion approach. However, it is preferred over iterative approach because of the simplicity.

> **Note:** The recursive function calls itself to solve a problem, but it may become an infinite loop (see Fig 5.2 (a)). To avoid infinite calling, we add the base case (Fig 5.2 (b)), which stops the recursive call when satisfied and returns the results.
>
> An exception will occur due to stack overflow if the base condition is not specified in recursion (This situation occurs when all the allocated space in a program is consumed by function calls.).

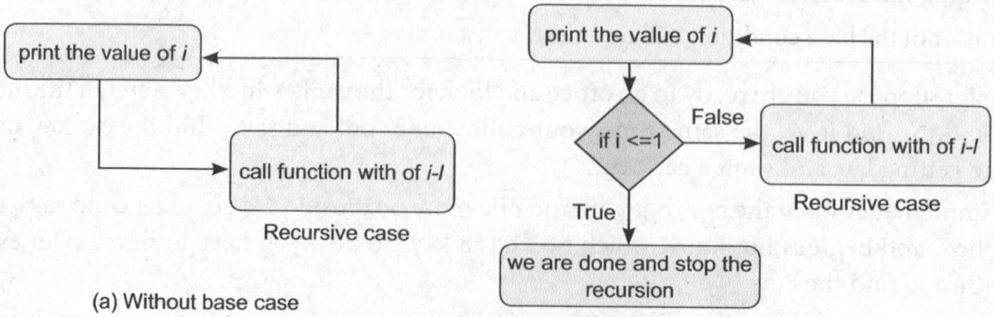

(a) Without base case

(b) With base case

Fig. 5.2: Representation of the base and recursive case

Let's take an example to calculate the factorial with the help of recursion in C programming.

```
1. #include<stdio.h>
2. int factNumbers(int);
3. int main()
4. {
5.    int varFact,varRes;
6.    printf("Enter a number to calculate factorial: ");
7.    scanf("%d",&varFact);

8.    varRes= factNumbers(varFact);
9.    printf("Factorial of %d = %d", varFact,varRes);
10.   return 0;
11. }

12. int factNumbers(int var)
13. {
14.   if (var>=1)
15.     return var*factNumbers(var-1);
16.   else
17.     return 1;
18. }
```

Fig. 5.3: Demonstration of the recursive function

Suppose the user entered 3 to calculate factorial. The function factNumbers(3) will call in line 8 (shown in Fig 5.3). The calling information of the function is stored in the stack structure (first come, last out), known as the *call -stack*. The top of the *call-stack* represents the latest function call. After meeting the base condition, each function will pop from the call stack and replace it with the return value. This process will continue until the *call-stack* does not empty. An illustration of the function calling with respect to the call stack is shown in Fig 5.4.

Output

```
Enter a number to calculate factorial: 3
Factorial of 3 = 6
```

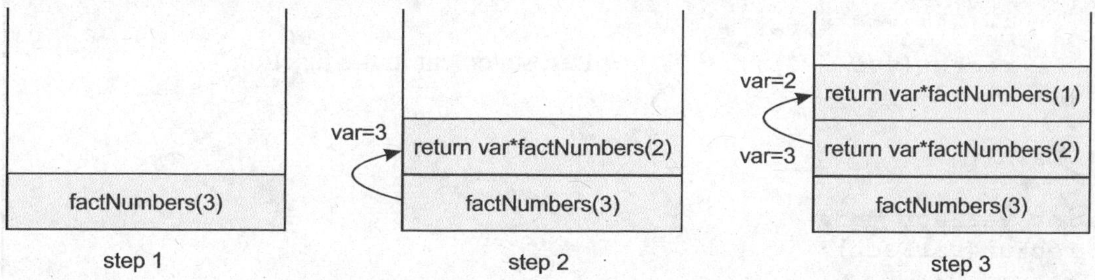

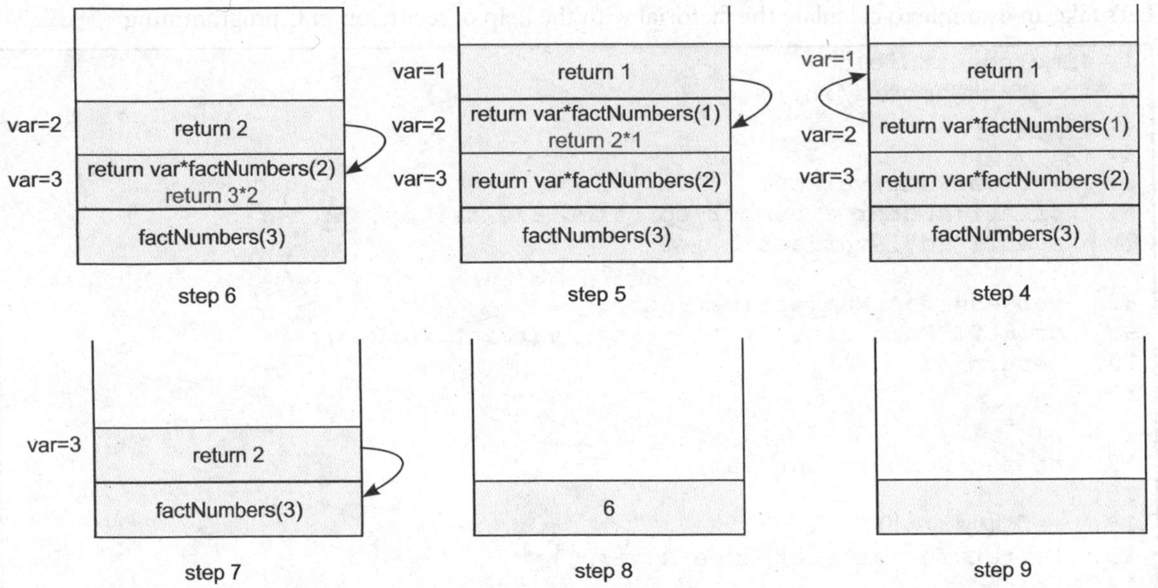

Fig. 5.4: Step-by-step working of the recursive function

5.2 TYPES OF RECURSIONS

Recursion is divided into two types: direct recursion and indirect recursion.

5.2.1 Direct Recursion

When a function call itself directly is known as direct recursion. Direct recursion is also further divided into four types.

(a) Tail recursion

In the tail recursion, the recursive call statement is written at last. Nothing is left to execute after the recursive call in the tail recursion (shown in Fig 5.5).

```
#include<stdio.h>
void recFun(int var)
{
    if (var1 > 0)
    {
        printf("%d ",var);
        recFun(var - 1);            // Last statement in the function
    }
}
int main()
{
    int varFact = 3;
    recFun(varFact);
    return 0;
}
```

Fig. 5.5: Demonstration of the tail recursion

Output

```
3 2 1
```

(b) Head recursion

In the head recursion, the recursion call statement is written as the first statement (shown in Fig 5.6).

```
#include<stdio.h>
void recFun(int var1)
{
  if (var1 > 0)
  {
    recFun(var1 - 1);          // First statement in the function
    printf("%d ",var1);
  }
}
int main()
{
    int varFact = 3;
    recFun(varFact);
    return 0;
}
```

Fig. 5.6: Demonstration of the head recursion

Output

```
1 2 3
```

(c) Linear and tree recursion

If a recursive function calls itself only one time, then it is known as linear recursion. If a recursive call executes more than one time is known as the tree recursion.

```
#include<stdio.h>
void recFun(int varFact)
{
  if (varFact > 0)
  {
    printf("%d ",varFact);
    recFun(varFact - 1);          // Calling once
    recFun(varFact - 1);          // Calling twice
  }
}

int main()
{
  int varFact = 3;
  recFun(varFact);
  return 0;
}
```

Fig. 5.7: Demonstration of the tree recursion

Lines 7 and 8 both are called the function recursively (shown in Fig 5.7)

Output

```
3 2 1 1 2 1 1
```

(d) Nested recursion

When a recursive function passes the parameter as the recursive call is known as nested recursion.

```
1.  #include <stdio.h>
2.  int nestedRecursion(int var)
3.  {
4.    if (var > 90)
5.      return var - 6;
6.    else
7.      return nestedRecursion(nestedRecursion(var + 7)); //Nested recursion
8.  }
9.  int main ()
10. {
11.     int var1 = 65;
12.     printf ("Result= %d", nestedRecursion(var1));
13.     return 0;
14. }
```

Fig. 5.8: Demonstration of the nested recursion

In the above example, line number 7 (shown in Fig 5.8) shows the nested recursion where `nestedRecursion()` function calls by the argument (parameter) `nestedRecursion()`.

Output

```
Result= 85
```

5.2.2 Indirect Recursion

In this type of recursion more than one function call to each other in a circular manner. In Fig 5.9 we can clearly see that, `recFunction1` calls `recFunction2`, `recFunction2` calls `recFunction3`, and `recFunction3` calls `recFunction1` which is the circular call. So, we can say the `recFunction1` call itself indirectly. The demonstration of the indirect recursion is shown in Fig 5.10.

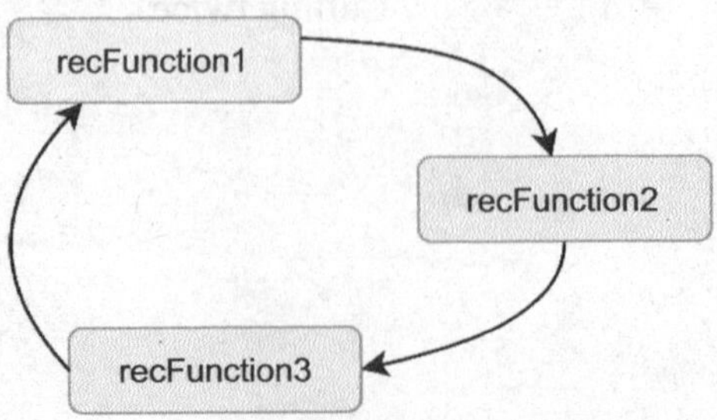

Fig. 5.9: Graphical representation of the indirect recursion

```c
#include <stdio.h>
void recFun1(int var1)
{
  if (var1 > 0)
  {
    printf("%d  ", var1);
    recFun1(var1 - 2);
  }
}
void recFun2(int var2)
{
  if(var2 > 0)
  {
    printf("%d ", var2);
    recFun2(var2 - 1);
  }
}
int main ()
{
  int var = 10;
  recFun1 (var);
  return 0;
}
```

Fig. 5.10: Demonstration of the indirect recursion

Output

```
10 8 6 4 2
```

5.3 RECURSIVE SOLUTIONS

Many of the classical problems are solved by the recursion technique. Here we are going to discuss some basic problems that are solved using recursion.

5.3.1 Factorial

Factorial is a basic problem that is solved by recursion. In that, we create a recursive function that calculates the multiplication of the two numbers. Here, the first operand will be the received number, and the second operand will be returned by the recursively called function (Recursive function called by a number -1).

Pseudocode (recursive):

function `factNumbers` **is:**

input: integer number `var` **such that** `var >= 0`

output: `[var × (var-1) × (var-2) × ... × 1]`

```
   1. if var>=1, return [var × factorial(var-1)]
   2. otherwise, return 1

end factNumbers
```

The demonstration of the factorial problem using the C programming language is already discussed in Fig 5.3.

5.3.2 Towers of Hanoi

A tower of Hanoi is a mathematical puzzle which solved using the recursion technique. In that, we have numerous disks with different sizes. Initially, all disks are stacked in one peg. We have to calculate the minimum number of steps to move the whole stack into another peg. The rule is that the larger disk cannot be stacked over the smaller disk, and at a time, only one disk can be moved. The diagrammatic view of the Tower of Hanoi is shown in Fig 5.11.

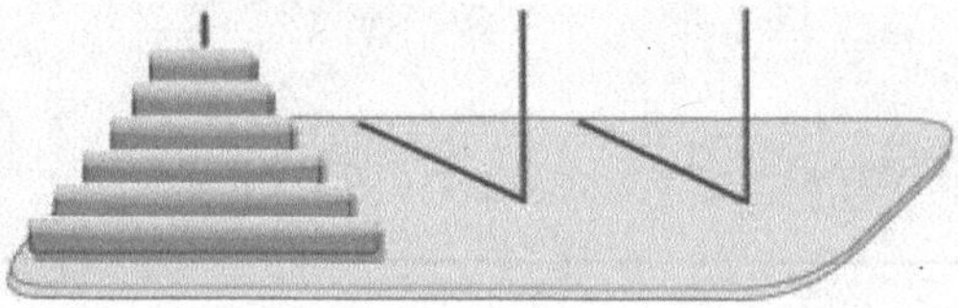

Fig. 5.11: Tower of Hanoi

Pseudocode (recursive):

```
function tower_Hanoi is:

input: integer var, such that var >= 1

   1. if var is 1 then return 1
   2. Otherwise return [2 * [tower_Hanoi (var-1)] + 1]

end tower_Hanoi
```

Fig 5.12 shows the demonstration of the Tower of Hanoi using the C programming language. In that, we can see line 7 recursively call the function `tower_Hanoi,` which tells the movement of the disk from one peg to another.

```
1.  #include <stdio.h>
2.  void tower_Hanoi(int var, char f_peg, char t_peg, char a_peg)
3.  {
4.     if (var == 1)
5.     {
         printf("\n Move disk 1 from peg %c to peg %c", f_peg, t_peg);
         return 0;
```

```
    }
    tower_Hanoi(var-1, f_peg, a_peg, t_peg);
    printf("\n Move disk %d from peg %c to peg %c",var,f_peg,t_peg);
    tower_Hanoi(var-1, a_peg, t_peg, f_peg);
}

int main()
{
    int var = 4;      // count of disks
    tower_Hanoi(var, 'X', 'Y', 'Z');     // X, Y and Z are names of pegs
    return 0;
}
```

Fig. 5.12: Demonstration of the Tower of Hanoi

Output

```
Move disk 1 from peg X to peg Z
Move disk 2 from peg X to peg Y
Move disk 1 from peg Z to peg Y
Move disk 3 from peg X to peg Z
Move disk 1 from peg Y to peg X
Move disk 2 from peg Y to peg Z
Move disk 1 from peg X to peg Z
Move disk 4 from peg X to peg Y
Move disk 1 from peg Z to peg Y
Move disk 2 from peg Z to peg X
Move disk 1 from peg Y to peg X
Move disk 3 from peg Z to peg Y
Move disk 1 from peg X to peg Z
Move disk 2 from peg X to peg Y
Move disk 1 from peg Z to peg Y
```

5.3.3 Binary Search

A binary search tree is an algorithm to search for an element in the sorted array. In this technique, the search element is matched with the middle element of the array. If it is greater than the middle element, then the possibility of the elements belonging to the left of the middle will be zero, and the subsequent search will be performed between middle+1 and the last element. If the element is less than the middle, then the following search will be performed between the first and middle-1 elements. If both conditions are false, the element will equal the middle element, and the search will be finished. To divide the array from the middle, the recursive technique is used. So, we can say the binary search technique is a recursive base solution for the search. For example, suppose we have a sorted array containing 7 elements and want to search a 13. The graphical representation of the search 13 using the binary search is shown in Fig. 5.13.

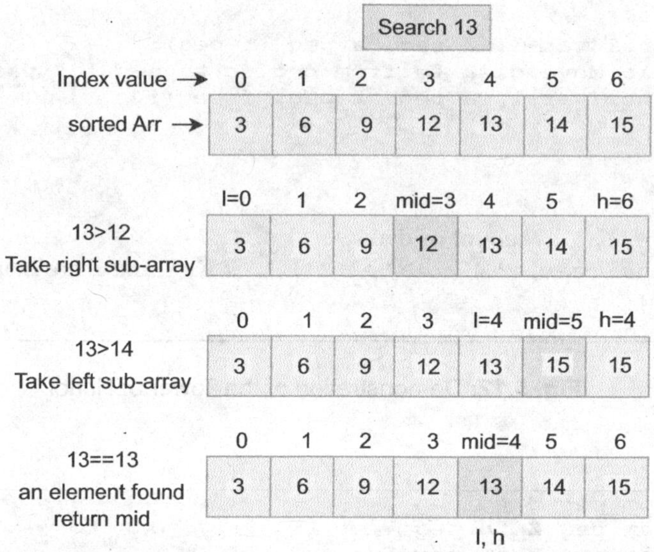

Fig. 5.13: Graphical representation of the binary search

Steps to search an element using a binary search algorithm:

Step 1: Initialize the sorted array

Step 2: Find the middle element of the array

Step 3: Match the middle element with the searched element (key)

if middle < key

drop the left side list of the middle and go back to step 2

if middle > key

drop the left side list of the middle and go back to step 2

else

return the index of the middle element and go to step 4

Step 4: End

```
#include <stdio.h>
int bSearch(int sortedArr[], int var1, int l, int h)
{
  if(h>=l)
  {
     int mid = l + (h - l) / 2;
     if (sortedArr[mid] == var1)
       return mid;
     if (sortedArr[mid] < var1)
       return bSearch(sortedArr,var1, mid + 1, h);

    return bSearch(sortedArr,var1, l, mid - 1);
```

```
12.     }
13.     return -1;
14. }

15. int main(void)
16. {
17.    int sortedArr[] = {3, 6, 9, 12, 13, 14, 15};
18.    int var, var1, varRes;
19.    var = sizeof(sortedArr) / sizeof(sortedArr[0]);
20.    printf("Enter element to be searched ");
21.    scanf("%d",&var1);

22.    varRes = bSearch(sortedArr, var1, 0, var-1 );
23.    if (varRes == -1)
24.      printf("Not found");
25.    else
26.      printf("Element is found at index %d", varRes);
27.    return 0;
28. }
```

Fig. 5.14: Demonstration of the Binary Search

In Fig 5.14, lines 10 and 11 are performed a recursive call that divides the array into two parts in every call. Let's suppose the user entered 13 and 6 elements to search.

Output

Question 5.1 How we can find Greatest Common Divisor of two integers using the recursion?

Scan QR for solution

```
Enter element to be searched 13
Element is found at index 4
```

```
Enter element to be searched 6
Element is found at index 1
```

UNIT SUMMARY

Introduction

- When a function calls itself (directly or indirectly), then it is known as the recursion in the C programming language.
- Recursion is a technique that breaks complex problems into small subproblems.

Types of recursions

- *There are two types of recursion, Direct recursion and Indirect recursion.*
- ***Direct recursion,*** *when a function calls itself directly, is known as direct recursion. It is further divided into four types: Tail recursion, Head recursion, Linear and tree recursion, and Nested recursion.*
    - *In the tail recursion, the recursive call statement is written at last.*
    - *In the head recursion, the recursive call statement is written as a first statement.*
    - *If a recursive function calls itself only once, it is known as linear recursion, and if it executes more than one time is known as tree recursion.*
    - *In nested recursion, a recursive function passes the parameter as a recursive call.*
- *In* ***Indirect recursion****, more than one function circularly calls to each other.*

Recursive Solutions

- *We solved some classical problems using the recursion technique.*
    - ***Factorial*** *is a basic problem that is solved by recursion. We create a recursive function that calculates the multiplication of the two numbers.*
    - ***A tower of Hanoi*** *is a mathematical puzzle that is solved using the recursion technique. Initially, all disks are stacked in one peg. We have to calculate the minimum number of steps to move the whole stack into another peg.*
    - ***A binary search tree*** *is an algorithm to search for an element in the sorted array. The recursive technique is used to divide an array from the middle.*

EXERCISES

Multiple Choice Questions

1. To store the information of the recursive call, which data structure is used?
   (a) queue (b) stack (c) array (d) None of these
2. A recursive function without base condition becomes an ___________.
   (a) Normal function (b) Infinite loop
   (c) Finite loop (d) None of these

3. Which type of problem will not solve by the recursion?
   (a) Tower of Hanoi
   (b) Greatest common divisor
   (c) Problems without base case
   (d) None of these
4. If more than one function calls one and another in a circular way, then it is known as __________.
   (a) Indirect recursive
   (b) Direct recursive
   (c) Two-way recursion
   (d) None of these
5. Which one is true in respect of the recursion?
   (a) Recursion provides the simple way to provide the solution
   (b) Stack data structure is used to call the recursive function
   (c) Recursion requires more memory than an iterative function
   (d) All of these

ANSWERS									
1.	(b)	2.	(b)	3.	(c)	4.	(a)	5.	(d)

Output-based Questions

What will be the output of the following programs?

A

```
#include <stdio.h>
void recFun(int var)
{
    if(var > 0)
    {
        recFun(--var);
        printf("%d",var);
        recFun(var--);
    }
}
int main()
{
    int var = 3;
    recFun(var);
    return 0;
}
```

B

```
#include<stdio.h>
recFunc(int var1)
{
  int var2;
  if(var1<=1)
    return 1;
  else
  var2=(var1+1)*recFunc(var1-1);
   return var2;
}
int main()
{
  int var;
  var=recFunc(5);
  printf("%d",var);
}
```

C

```
#include<stdio.h>
int main()
{
    int var;
    var=recFun(10);
    printf("%d",var);
}
int recFun(int var)
{
    if(var>0)
    {
        printf("HI");
        recFun(var--);
    }
    else
        return 0;
}
```

D

```
#include<stdio.h>
int recFun(int);
int main()
{
    int var=9;
    printf("%d",recFun(var));
}
int recFun(int var)
{
    if(var>0)
      return(var+recFun(var-2));
    else
        return 0;
}
```

E

```
#include<stdio.h>
void funRec(int var)
{
    if (var > 0)
    {
        funRec(var - 2);
        printf("%d ",var);
        funRec(var - 2);
    }
}
int main()
{
    funRec(4);
    return 0;
}
```

F

```
#include<stdio.h>
int recFun(int var1, int var2)
{
if(var1==0)
  return 0;
else
  return recFun(var1/2, 2*var2)-
var2;
}
int main()
{
printf("%d",recFun(1,2));
return 0;
}
```

Answers of Output-based Questions	
A. 0102010	B. 360
C. print HI infinite times	D. 25
E. 2 4 2	F. -2

Short and Long Answer Type Questions

1. Fill in the blanks
   (a) When a function calls itself, then it is known as the______________.
   (b) In the tail recursion, the recursive call statement is written at __________.
   (c) In an ____________ recursion, two or more functions call each other in a circular manner.
   (d) When a recursive function passes the parameter as the recursive call is known as the ____________ recursion
   (e) It is a ____________ recursion if the recursive function calls itself more than one time.

Answers			
(a) recursion	(b) last	(c) indirect	(d) nested
(e) tree			

PRACTICAL

1. Write a program to ask the user to enter an integer number and perform the following operations using recursion:
   (a) Count the total number of digits present in a number.
   (b) Count the sum of even digits of the number.
   (c) Count the sum of the odd digits of the number.
   (d) Count the sum and average of all the digits of a number.
2. Write a program to print the Fibonacci series using the recursion where the number of the terms to be printed will be entered by the user.
3. Using the recursion, write a program to check whether an entered number is a palindrome or not. (Hint: `23432` is a palindrome while `23231` is not)
4. Create a C program that uses recursion to convert a decimal number into binary.
5. Create an array of size `n`; find all possible combinations of the `m` elements in the array and print them.
6. For example: suppose entered array is `{2,4,6,8}` and the value of m is `2` then the output should be `{2,4}`, `{2,6}`, `{2,8}`, `{4,6}`, `{4,8}`, and `{6,8}`.

KNOW MORE

Command line arguments

In the C programming language, the most important function is the *main()* function. The compiler always looks to execute whatever is written or referenced inside the main function. In most of the programs, the main function is defined without arguments.

```
int main()
{
  /* code... */
}
```

We can also write the main function with arguments, which are known as command-line arguments. With the command line arguments, the main function is defined using two arguments. The first argument keeps the count of the passed arguments, and the second one is the pointer-type array, which refers to each passed argument. Command line arguments are given after the program's name in the command line.

Definition of the main function using the command line arguments:

```
int main(int argcount, char * argvalue[])
{
  /* code...   */
}
```

or

```
int main(int argcount, char ** argvalue)
{
  /* code...   */
}
```

Here `argcount` is used to store the count of the passed arguments, including the program's name, and `argvalue` is used to store the given (passed) data. If the value of `argcount` is greater than 0, then the array `argvalue` (from `argvalue[0]` to `argvalue[argcount-1]`) contains pointer to string. The first block of the array contains the name of the program (`argvalue[0]`), and other blocks from `argvalue[1]` to `argvalue[argcount-1]` contain the list of the entered arguments. Run the following code on the Linux machine.

```
#include <stdio.h>
int main(int argcount, char *argvalue[])
{
   printf("The value of argcount is: %d\n",argcount);
   if(argcount >= 2)
{
      printf("Value in first block %s\n", argvalue[0]);
      printf("The supplied arguments:\n");
      for (int i=1; i<argcount;i++)
     {
         printf("%s\n", argvalue[i]);
      }
   }
   else
```

```
15.     {
16.         printf("at least one argument required.\n");
17.     }
18.     return 0;
19. }
```

Fig. 5.15: Demonstration of the command line arguments

In the above example (Fig 5.15), we have used command line arguments received in line 2. Now, we compile the code on the Linux machine, which generates an object file (`a.out`), and to run the code, we use the command `./a.out` followed by `I am a programmer` (command line argument).

Commands are written for the execution of the above code:

```
$gcc FileName.c     // a.out file will create after the successful compilation
$./a.out I am a programmer
```

Output:

```
The value of argcount is: 5
Value in first block ./a.out
The supplied arguments:
I
am
a
programmer
```

REFERENCES AND SUGGESTED READINGS

1. Deitel, P. J. (2015). *C how to Program: With an Introduction to C++ (**Chapter** 5).* Pearson Education India.
2. David Griffiths and Dawn Griffiths (2011). Head First C, O'Reilly Media, Inc
3. https://nptel.ac.in/courses/106104128
4. https://nptel.ac.in/courses/106105171 *(week 8 video lectures)*

Dynamic QR Code for Further Reading

The author has created supporting video lectures for each unit. Readers are encouraged to watch the lectures to better understand the topics covered in Unit V. However, it is advised to read the book units first and then see the videos. The video lectures may not cover the whole unit but are provided as supplementary material.

APPENDICES

APPENDIX-A

Standard Library Functions

Standard library functions are predefined and can be used by including the respected library in the program. In the book, we have already discussed some basic library (predefined) functions like printf(), scanf(), gets(), and puts(). Books based on C programming can not be completed without the library functions. C programming has too many library functions, and all of these are not possible to discuss here. This section includes the most popular and used standard library functions with the sort description. There are some dedicated books for all library functions, like Waite group's, Turbo C Bible, written by Nabjyoti Barkakti.

The standard library functions are classified into different categories. Following is the list of library functions based on the categories.

Arithmetic Functions

Function	System Include File	Description
pow	math.h	This function calculates the power of a value
exp	math.h	Calculate the exponential e to the nth power
abs	stdlib.h	Calculates an integer's absolute value
floor	math.h	Find out the largest integer number but less than the given float number.
fmod	math.h	Return the remainder of the float value
fabs	math.h	Calculate the absolute value
cos	math.h	Find the cosine of the given value
cosh	math.h	Find the hyperbolic cosine of the given arguments
log	math.h	Return the natural logarithm value
log10	math.h	Return the logarithm value by base 10
sqrt	math.h	Return the square root of the given value
tan	math.h	Return the tangent of the given arguments
tanh	math.h	Calculate the hyperbolic tangent of the passed argument
sin	math.h	Find the sine of the passed argument
sinh	math.h	Find the hyperbolic sine of the passed argument

Data Conversion Functions

Function	System Include File	Description
atoi	stdlib.h	Changes string to integer (int)
atof	stdlib.h	Changes string to float number (float)
atol	stdlib.h	Changes string to long

itoa	stdlib.h	Changes integer (int) to string
ltoa	stdlib.h	Changes long to string
ultoa	stdlib.h	Changes unsigned long to string
strtod	stdlib.h	Changes string to double
strtol	stdlib.h	Changes string to long integer (long int)
strtoul	stdlib.h	Changes string to unsigned long integer
fcvt	stdlib.h	Changes float value to string
gcvt	stdlib.h	Changes float value to string
ecvt	stdlib.h	Changes float value to string

Searching and Sorting Functions

Function	System Include File	Description
qsort	stdlib.h	Sort the given data using the quick sort algorithm
lfind	search.h	Search the given element using the linear search
bsearch	stdlib.h	Use the binary search to find the given number

String Manipulation Functions

Function	System Include File	Description
strcpy	string.h	Copies the source string into the destination string
strchr	string.h	Finds the first occurrence of the given character in a string
strcmp	string.h	Performs character-by-character comparison between two strings
strcmpi	string.h	Compares two given strings without care for the letter case.
strdup	string.h	Creates a new string, which is the duplicate of the given string
strlen	string.h	Finds the length (number of the characters) of the given string
strcat	string.h	Concatenates the given two string
strncpy	string.h	Copies up to n characters from the source string to the destination
strrev	string.h	Reverse the given string
strstr	string.h	Returns a pointer to the starting of the first occurrence of the second string within the first string
strupr	string.h	Converts the given string into the uppercase

I/O Functions

Function	System Include File	Description
fopen	stdio.h	Used to open or create a file with specific attributes like 'a', 'w', and 'r'
fclose	stdio.h	Used to close the file

fgetc	stdio.h	Used to read a character from the file
fgetchar	stdio.h	Used to read a character from the keyboard
fgets	stdio.h	Used to read a specific file line by line
fputs	stdio.h	Used to put lines of characters into the specific file
fscanf	stdio.h	Used to read formatted data from the file
fseek	stdio.h	Used to shift file pointer location to the specific place

APPENDIX-B

Creating Libraries

In C programming user can create its own libraries, which can contain several user-defined functions and can be used in the future. Let us suppose we want to create a library that contains some user-defined functions like `addNumber()`, `subNumber()`, `multiNumber()`, and `divNumber()`. As the name suggests, the functions `addNumber()`, `sunNumber()`, `multiNumber()`, and `divNumber()` perform the arithmetic operations (addition, subtraction, multi[plication, and division, respectively) and return the results. To create the library following are the steps to follow.

Note: The following process is for the Turbo C/C++ compiler. It can differ for the other compiler.

a) Create a file, say `my_functions.c` without `main` function and define the user defined functions `addNumber()`, `subNumber()`, `multiNumber()`, and `divNumber`.

b) Next create a new file with extension .h says `my_functions.h` and inside it declare all the used functions `addNumber()`, `subNumber()`, `multiNumber()`, and `divNumber()`. The declaration of the functions is shown below:

```
double addNumber(double, double);
double subNumber(double, double);
double multiNumber(double, double);
double  divNumber(double, double);
```

c) Go to the menu, and choose the menu-item 'Application'. The dialog box will pop up. Choose the 'Library' option and press OK.

d) To compile the file, press Alt F9. After the compilation, `my_functions.lib` library file will be created.

Now the library is ready to use. We can use all the functions defined inside the `my_functions.lib` library by including it in the program. Following are the steps to include the user-defined library and use their functions.

a) Create a new file with extension c say `fileName.c` and write the following code.

```
#include " my_functions.h "
main( )
{
```

```
    double resAdd, resMulti;

    resAdd = addNumber ( 20.5, 10.2 );
    resMulti = multiNumber ( 13.0, 5.0 );

    printf ( "Addition: %lf\n, resAdd);
    printf("Multiplication: %lf", resMulti);
}
```

Note: The file `my_functions.h` should be in the same directory as the file `filename.h`. If both files are in a different directory, then mention the proper path while including the my_functions.h header file.

b) Next to create a project, select "Open Project' from the project menu. The dialog box will appear. Write the project's name, say `projName.prj` and press OK.

c) Now select 'Add Item' from the 'project' menu. A file dialog box will pop up. To add the file in this project, choose the file `fileName.c` and elect 'Add'. Now follow the same process to add the library file `my_function.lib`. At the end press 'Done'.

d) To compile and run the project press `Ctrl F9`.

APPENDIX-C

List of suggested topics for practical

Sr. No	Topics for Practical
1	Familiarization with programming environment (Editor, Compiler, etc.)
2	Programs using I/O statements and various operators
3	Programs using expression evaluation and precedence
4	Programs using decision making statements and branching statements
5	Programs using loop statements
6	Programs to demonstrate applications of n dimensional arrays
7	Programs to demonstrate use of string manipulation functions
8	Programs to demonstrate parameter passing mechanism
9	Programs to demonstrate recursion
10	Programs to demonstrate use of pointers
11	Programs to demonstrate command line arguments
12	Programs to demonstrate dynamic memory allocation
13	Programs to demonstrate file operations

REFERENCES FOR FURTHER LEARNING

1. Lundqvist, I. Kristina. "Introduction to Computers and Programming." (2004).
2. B.L. Juneja and Anita Seth, Programming for Problem Solving (2019) Published by CENGAGE INDIA, 2019, ISBN 10: 9387994600ISBN.
3. Deitel, P.J., & Deitel, H. M. (2016). C: How to program; with an introduction to C++. Pearson.
4. R.S. Salaria, Programming for Problem Solving (All India). Khanna Publishing House, ISBN: 9789389139112, 2021.
5. Miller, Dean, and Perry, Greg. C Programming Absolute Beginner's Guide. United Kingdom, Pearson Education, 2013.
6. Ritchie, Dennis M., and Kernighan, BrianW.. The C programming. language India, Prentice Hall, 1988.
7. Balagurusamy, E.. Programming in ANSI C. India, McGraw Hill Education (India) Private Limited, 2019.
8. Yashavant P. Kanetkar. Let Us C, Eighth Edition (8th. ed.). Jones and Bartlett Publishers, Inc., USA, 2008.
9. Gottfried, Byron S.. Schaum's Outline of Programming with C. United Kingdom, McGraw-Hill Education, 1996.

CO AND PO ATTAINMENT TABLE

Course outcomes (COs) for this course can be mapped with the programme outcomes (POs) after the completion of the course and a correlation can be made for the attainment of POs to analyze the gap. After proper analysis of the gap in the attainment of POs necessary measures can be taken to overcome the gaps.

Table for CO and PO attainment

Course Outcomes	Attainment of Programme Outcomes (1- Weak Correlation; 2- Medium correlation; 3- Strong Correlation)						
	PO-1	PO-2	PO-3	PO-4	PO-5	PO-6	PO-7
CO-1							
CO-2							
CO-3							
CO-4							
CO-5							
CO-6							

The data filled in the above table can be used for gap analysis.

INDEX

A

Addition, 4, 17, 19, 29
Alphanumeric, 14
AMD, 10
AND operator, 27, 32
Arg_list, 115
Arithmetic, 4, 8, 27, 29
Arithmetic Operators, 28, 44
Array, 99, 100, 101
Assembly language, 7, 20
Assignment, 27, 28, 55
Assignment Operators, 28, 29, 30
Associativity, 26, 27, 42
asterisk (*), 106, 127
Auto, 10, 13, 124

B

Basic elements, 12
Binary Operators, 27, 28
Binary search, 143, 145
Bitwise Operator, 28, 34
Break, 146

C

C programming, 2, 8, 9, 13
Calculator, 19, 74, 84, 85
Call by Reference, 118, 119, 128
Call by value, 128
Calling, 99, 105, 114, 116, 118
Calloc(), 105, 108
Char, 14, 15, 22, 150
Char (signed), 15
Character constant, 14
Code Editor, 9
Code reusability, 114, 124, 128
Column-major, 113
Compiler, 8, 9, 10
Computational thinking, 1, 2, 3, 19
Computer memory, 5, 6, 19, 103
Computing devices, 4
Conditional operator, 27, 40, 60
Constant, 13, 14, 101, 103,
Continue statement, 82, 83
Control Instruction, 27
Control Statements, 62, 64
CPU, 5, 9, 10

D

Data Types, 100, 102
Decision, 30, 65
Declaration, 99, 101, 102
Declarative knowledge, 3, 19
Declaration, 8, 16, 99
Decrement of a pointer, 107
Direct recursion, 138
Division, 28, 44
Double, 50, 100, 101
Do-while loop, 76, 80,

E

Eclipse, 10
Entry control loop, 76
Escape sequence, 49, 50, 56
Execution, 9, 12, 18, 64

Exit control loop, 80
Explicit-type, 40
Extern, 4, 13, 104

F

Factorial, 88, 137, 141, 146
Fclose, 52, 53, 56, 153
Field width, 46, 50
File, 52, 53
FILO, 105
First Program, 11
Float, 56, 100
Flowline, 97
Fopen, 52, 53
For loop, 76, 78, 103
Function name, 114, 115
Function, 10, 12, 17
Function Calling, 99, 105, 118
Function body, 128

G

Goto, 88

H

Head recursion, 139, 146
Heap, 104, 105

I

Identifiers, 13, 28
IDEs, 10
If statement, 65, 66
If-else, 67, 68
If-else-if, 70
Imperative knowledge, 3, 19
Implicit, 40, 41
Increment operator, 38
Indirect recursion, 134, 140
Initialized data segment, 104, 127
Inner loop, 87
Input-Output, 12, 26
Instructions, 1, 3, 4, 6, 8
Int, 23
Int (signed), 15
Intel microprocessor, 6

K

Keywords, 9, 13

L

LIFO, 105
Linear, 113
Loader, 10
Logical NOT, 34
Logical Operator, 27, 28, 31, 32

M

Machine language, 6, 7, 20
Malloc(), 105
MATLAB, 7, 61
Memory, 5
Memory allocation, 103, 105, 127
Memory Organization, 127
Modulo Operator, 19, 103
Multidimensional Array, 111, 128
Multiple-line comments, 12
Multiplication, 28, 29, 43

N

Naming Rules, 16
Natural language, 7, 20

Nested if-else, 70
Nested loop, 86
Nested recursion, 140
NOT operator, 34
Null Pointer, 108, 109
Numeric, 14

O

Operators in C, 26, 27, 42, 55
OR operator, 33
Outer loop, 87

P

Passing Array, 122
Pointers, 107, 108, 127
Post-decrement, 37, 39
Post-increment, 39
Precedence, 26, 42
Precision, 50
Pre-decrement, 37, 38
Pre-define Function, 17
Preprocessor, 9
Primary expression, 27
Printf, 27, 51, 53
Printing characters, 49, 59
Printing strings, 49
Process, 75, 97
Product, 29
Program_file, 53, 54
Programming, 95
Pseudocode, 141, 142

R

Realloc(), 105
Recursion, 134, 138
Register, 13, 126, 142
Relational Operator, 28, 30
Reminder, 29, 98
Repetition, 62, 64
Representation in an array, 103
Return data_type, 115, 116
Row-major, 113

S

Scanf, 10, 12, 17
Selection Statement, 62, 64, 65
Semantic, 8
Separators, 13
Short int (signed), 15
Single-line comments, 12
Sizeof, 13, 37, 107
Stack, 127
Statics Semantic, 8
Static, 8, 124
Stdio.h, 130, 148
Storage classes, 99, 124, 128
Stored address, 106, 127
Stored program, 4
String as Array, 109, 128
String constant, 14
Subtraction, 28
Summation, 29
Switch, 73
Syntax, 74, 77, 83, 88

T

Tail recursion, 138
Terminal, 97
Ternary Operator, 40, 69

Text segment, 104
Towers of Hanoi, 142
Tree recursion, 139, 146
Turbo C, 10, 152

U

Unary minus, 36, 37
Unary Operator, 27, 34, 36
Unary plus, 36
Uninitialized data segment, 104, 127
Unsigned char, 15
Unsigned int, 15, 22
Unsigned long int, 22, 153

V

Variables, 8, 13, 15
Visual Studio, 10
Void, 15
Void pointer, 120

W

While loop, 77
Wild pointer, 108, 109